It's All in the Name

It's All in the Name

Keith Brovald

Rev. date: 08/28/2017

To order additional copies of this book, contact:
Xlibris
1-888-795-4274
www.Xlibris.com
Orders@Xlibris.com
766756

Table of Contents

DEDICATION

I would like to dedicate this book to my lovely fiancé Maria.

FOREWORD

What you are about to discover within these contents is the result of various information accumulated over an extended period of time by a somewhat impractical individual with an unusually bizarre imagination. In fact, it all began on the morning of Sunday, August 26, 1979. For it was on that day that I was introduced to what would quickly become my all time favorite hobby. One which I affectionately call, "It's All In The Name". You may possibly wonder how I can pinpoint the actual day of origin this many years after the fact. Such curiosity would be legitimate and skepticism in any form is understandable. But I am able to say this with total certainty and I assure you that the start date and time is absolutely correct, give or take twenty to thirty minutes or so.

As I look back in time, the summer of 1979 was when two of my best friends, Mike and Rick, had made plans to accompany me on a weekend gambling trip. Since they were both three years my elder, the only thing we needed to be Reno bound, was for my twenty first birthday to take place. That it did, as I became society legal on August 19, 1979. The very next Friday, August 24th, we left Eugene and headed for Nevada with money to play and, as it turned out, money to lose. Two days later, on August 26th, we headed for home. The drive would take approximately eight hours and be nothing more than routine. Or so we thought. During this journey home however, there was an added element that made the trip a little more interesting. As it turned out, it was perhaps the most eventful eight hours of my entire life. A moment in time that I will never forget.

We hit the road out of Reno somewhere around 9:00 A.M. Rick took the wheel, allowing Mike to ride shotgun. Since I had the back seat entirely to myself, my initial plan was to hopefully shorten the trip by sleeping as much as possible. On this day of travel however, sleep would not be an option and little did I know that within the next hour, my life was going to change slightly. In a very good way. It all started as we were approaching the halfway point to Susanville, about fifty miles north of Reno. I can still recall the following sequence of events and how they played out:

As laughter spilled out of his mouth, Rick looked at Mike, glanced back my way, and said, "I know, let's think of names. I'll go first. Jim Nasium." Then Mike made eye contact with me before stating, "Oh, I get it.............I'll go with Bob Sled." There was a slight moment of silence as I pondered the situation. Just fifteen seconds ago I was about as horizontal as one can be in the backseat of a Buick Sky Hawk. Under normal circumstances during freeway ventures, I would have remained in such a backseat posture. But this was not a normal circumstance. My mind was now racing and it was doing its best to tell me that we were on to something here. I could sense that this particular something had the potential to be really big. Consequently, I was now fully upright. Very much at attention and ready to participate. Deductive reasoning indicated that it should now be my turn. Without further hesitation, I took part in the diversion. "How 'bout this guys?" I questioned. "I choose Foster Holmes and Adam Baum." I said. Rick and Mike nodded there approval as the three of us began laughing in unison. It was now official. The original four charter members of "It's All In The Name" were firmly in place. My next move was to reach into my duffle bag for some notebook paper and a writing instrument. I wasn't about to let this opportunity slip by. I immediately appointed myself as "the keeper of the names".

For the remainder of the drive home, the three of us continuously came up with new names similar in nature. Names which people could theoretically have while also holding a separate meaning all in itself. In retrospect, the list was approaching triple figures as we reached Eugene and went our separate ways, effectively bringing an end to the beginning of "The Names". During that trip home however, the foundation had been set and "The Names" were ready to thrive. From that moment on, I had a jewel of a toy to play with, and I knew it. I simply took off running with it, never looking back. I've been adding new entries ever since.

Nearly forty years have now passed since that fateful Sunday morning. As one might have guessed, the contents within "It's All In The Name" has become a fully grown beast, substantially larger than during it's days of infancy as well as becoming categorically in order. With a never ending ability to grow, this is truly a most remarkable species.

You are hereby invited to toy with "It's All In The Name".

Keith A. Brovald

PRELUDE

As you look through the individual entries within the contents of "It's All In The Name", keep a few things in mind. For starters, the list of names includes over 2,500, with no two being identical. They are listed by category with over fifty different classifications. Although the majority of the names could easily qualify for presentation under two or more of these headings, every individual name is represented only once throughout the listings. Their classification placement is based solely on the opinion of one individual…..me.

A few rules pertain to "It's All In The Name" as well. Since it is my book, it also comes with my rules. All entries are entirely first and last names only. There are no middle initials or abbreviations used of any kind. In addition, three specific first names are not allowed within these lists. You will not find the names of Betty, Kenny and Willie as a first name anywhere within this publication. Such names are too easy to run with. After all, we are still using my rules, remember. There are also separate rules specifically pertaining to the eligibility of first and last names. For a first name to receive eligibility, it must be considered authentic by method of documentation somewhere within the history of mankind. Nicknames consequently, become eligible. For instance. "Skip Rope and Slim Chance" are legitimate. And finally, the abiding rule for last names is relatively simple. Keep it to four syllables or less.

So, there you have it. All-in-all, it's really not that difficult. However, one thing is virtually guaranteed if you so choose to continue beyond this point. You will unquestionably become highly tempted to create your own additions to the list of those already in place. And, if I might add, there is no doubt whatsoever that you will be successful in doing so.

This never ending journey is now firmly in your hands. It has officially become part of your life. Enjoy the ride and welcome aboard.

SO MANY THINGS TO SAY

Communication & Media

ORIGIN OF NAME	NAME TO BE
I'll listen, you speak	Allison Ewspeek
I'll listen to you	Allison Tooya
A man delivering mail	Amanda Livringmale
Answering	Ann Surring
Beeping	Bea Ping
Buzzing	Buzz Zing
Called well ahead	Caldwell LaHead
Syndicate	Cinda Kate
Cordless phone	Cord Lesfone
Daily news	Dailey Nues
Daily paper	Dailey Payper
Database	Data Base
Dictation	Dick Tation
Dot com	Dot Comm
Dot matrix	Dot Maytrix
Editor	Ed Didder
Editing	Edda Ting
Editorial	Edda Toryull
Hinting	Hind Ting
Coding	Ko Ding
Call you later	Kolya Laidurr
List her number	Lister Number
Modulate	Maude Julate
More reason to speak	Maurice Undaspeak
Mailing	Maye Ling
Memory banks	Memory Banks
Microsoft	Mike Krowsoft
Paging	Paige Jingh
Film at eleven	Phil Madolevin

P.O. Box	**Pio Box**
Rating	**Ray Ting**
Reason to speak	**Reece Undaspeak**
Roger Houston	**Roger Houston**
Roger Over	**Roger Over**
Sent a memo	**Senta Memo**
Sent a message	**Senta Message**
Cyber net	**Sy Burnett**
Typing	**Ty Ping**

Declarations & Confirmations

ORIGIN OF NAME	NAME TO BE
Able to	**Abel Tu**
I'll be back	**Albie Back**
I'll be down	**Albie Down**
I'll be there	**Albie Thair**
I'll be willing	**Albie Willing**
I'll expect you	**Alex Spekcha**
I'll see you later (speech impediment)	**Althea Laidurr**
I'll see you there (speech impediment)	**Althea Thair**
I'll see you soon (speech impediment)	**Althea Thoon**
Adios	**Audie Ose**
Boasting	**Beau Sting**
Carry on	**Carrie Awn**
Chance you take	**Chance Yuhtake**
Close enough	**Cloe Synnuff**
Count me in	**Count Meeyin**
Day me and you left	**Damian Ewleft**
Day me and you met	**Damian Ewmeht**
I lean to the left	**Eileen Toudaleft**

I lean to the right	**Eileen Toudawright**
I lean your way	**Eileen Yorway**
You'll agree	**Eula Gree**
Ever since I met her	**Everson Ciemehter**
Ever since we met	**Everson Sweemeht**
Fair assessment	**Farrah Cessment**
Frankly	**Frank Lee**
Heard a good one	**Herta Goodwin**
Heard enough	**Herta Nuff**
Hindsight	**Hines Site**
Hope to see you	**Hope Taseeya**
I'd have beat her	**Ida Beadurr**
I'd have done it	**Ida Dunnitt**
I'd have kissed her	**Ida Kister**
I'd have quit	**Ida Quit**
I'd have tried	**Ida Tride**
I respect you	**Ira Spekcha**
Just in case	**Justin Caisse**
Just another one	**Justin Notherwun**
Just in time	**Justin Tyme**
Meet you later	**Micha Laidurr**
Meet you there	**Micha Thair**
More to come along	**Morta Kummalong**
Over here	**Ova Heer**
Over there	**Ova Thair**
Realistic	**Rhea Listic**
Write her off	**Ryder Roff**
Surely I'm right	**Shirley Imwright**
Slick as ice	**Slick Kuhzice**
It's all good now	**Sol Goodnow**
Tiny bit	**Tiny Bitt**
Tough break	**Tuff Braike**
You'd have beat her	**Yuda Beadurr**

You'd have done it	**Yuda Dunnitt**
You'd have quit	**Yuda Quit**
You'd have tried	**Yuda Tride**
You the one	**Yuda Wahn**
You'll be sorry	**Yuell BeSahry**

Appreciating Others

ORIGIN OF NAME	**NAME TO BE**
Able body	**Abel Bottie**
Aide a black man	**Aida Blackman**
I'll do it	**Al Duit**
I'll listen in	**Allison Inn**
A meal and a cot	**Amile Endicott**
Bear hug	**Bear Hugg**
Best wishes	**Bess Wishes**
Bid adieu	**Bid Adeu**
Bid farewell	**Bid Fairwell**
Buddy old pal	**Buddy Olepal**
Buddy system	**Buddy System**
Buddy up	**Buddy Yupp**
Care enough	**Cara Nuff**
Charity auction	**Charity Auction**
Count on it	**Count Tawnit**
Day to remember	**Data Remehmbir**
I lean on you	**Eileen Onyu**
Grace period	**Grace Period**
Granting	**Grant Ting**
Guiding	**Guy Ding**
Holding up	**Holden Nupp**
Honor system	**Honor System**
Hi there	**Hy Thair**
Gerrymander	**Jerry Mander**

Wanting	**Juan Ting**
Want to be friends?	**Juana BeFrenze**
Caring about you	**Karen Abouchu**
Lean on me	**Lee Nonmee**
Lend me a hand	**Len Miahan**
Let's be friends	**Les BeFrenze**
Maximize	**Max Simize**
Maximum	**Max Symum**
Noticing	**Nota Singh**
Raking	**Ray King**
Reassuring	**Rhea Shurring**
Rendering	**Rhen Durring**
Salvaging	**Sal Veging**
Tipping	**Tip Ping**
Tip her generously	**Tipper Jennrussly**
UNICEF	**Una Seff**
Way to go	**Wade Duhgohe**
Winds her over	**Windsor Rover**
Utilize	**Yuda Lies**

Personal Actions

ORIGIN OF NAME	NAME TO BE
I'll beat off	**Albie Doff**
Bating	**Bae Ting**
Beat off	**Bea Doff**
Blew it out	**Blue Idtout**
Booting	**Boo Ting**
Bumped into it	**Bump Intuit**
Chatterbox	**Chad Errbox**
Crashed out	**Crash Dout**
I lean into it	**Eileen Nintuit**
Faker	**Faye Kerr**

Faking	**Faye King**
Halting	**Hall Ting**
How evasive	**Howie Vaisive**
Hung out	**Hung Out**
Hiding	**Hy Ding**
Jacked off	**Jack Doff**
Gesture	**Jess Churr**
Join her	**Joy Nurr**
Wandering	**Juan Durring**
Knocks on doors	**Knox Sondoors**
Lean up	**Lee Nupp**
Leaving	**Lee Ving**
Leave early	**Lee Vurly**
Less moody	**Les Moody**
Less stern	**Les Stern**
Light a match	**Lida Match**
Mingling	**Ming Gling**
Pat your ass	**Pat Churrass**
Patting	**Pat Ting**
Picked out	**Pic Dout**
Picked up	**Pic Dupp**
Picking	**Pic King**
Pop in	**Pop Pihn**
Realize	**Rhea Lies**
Reacquaint	**Rhea Quaint**
Rolled over	**Roald Dover**
Rolling around	**Roland Rown**
Skipped out	**Skip Dout**
Skipped over	**Skip Dover**
Slide over	**Sly Dover**
Slide under	**Sly Dunder**
Stand and deliver	**Stan Dendeliver**
Stand over	**Stan Dover**

Starting	**Starr Ting**
Sticking	**Stic King**
Taker	**Taye Kerr**
Taking	**Taye King**
Tear them up	**Terra Mupp**
Turn her into it	**Turner Rintuitt**
Waiting	**Waite Ting**
Walk her into it	**Walker Rintuitt**
Wheel her out	**Wheeler Out**
Wheel her over	**Wheeler Rover**

Figure Of Speech

ORIGIN OF NAME	NAME TO BE
I'll be damned	**Al BeDamned**
Baker's dozen	**Bake Erzdozen**
Blue moon	**Blue Moon**
Buck oh	**Buck Oh**
Candy ass	**Candi Asc**
Cookie crumbles	**Cookie Crumbulls**
Day to day	**Data Daye**
The one and only	**DeJuan Enoanly**
Diamond in the rough	**Diamond Dintheruff**
Hell if I know	**Ella Finoe**
Every now and then	**Evy Nowenthen**
Fair and square	**Faron Square**
Fair is fair	**Farris Fair**
Frankly speaking	**Frank Leaspeaking**
Grace under fire	**Grace Sunderfire**
Hanky panky	**Hank Keepankey**
Happy go lucky	**Happy Goalucky**
Hardy harhar	**Hardie Harhar**
Heidi ho	**Heidi Hoe**
Hell to pay	**Helda Paye**

Hell and back	**Helen Back**
Hell in a hand basket	**Helena Hanbasket**
Hell on wheels	**Helen Wheels**
Heard it all	**Herta Dahl**
I've an inkling	**Ivan Ninkling**
Jack of all trades	**Jack Kovalltraids**
Jerryrigg	**Jerry Rigg**
Jimmyrigg	**Jimmy Rigg**
You only live once	**Jouni Livwunce**
Knocks on wood	**Knox Sawnwood**
Lady luck	**Lady Luck**
Lie like a dog	**Lila Kuhdawg**
Living large	**Liv Enlarge**
Live and let live	**Liv Enletlive**
Live it up	**Liv Vitdupp**
Loose cannon	**Lou Scannon**
Low and behold	**Lowen BeHold**
Mows them over	**Mose Zemover**
Nick knack	**Nick Nak**
Know it all	**Noah Dahl**
Okie dokie	**Oak Keedoaky**
All he could stand for	**Ollie Coodstanfore**
Oh my god	**Oma Gawd**
Oh so simple (speech impediment)	**Otho Thinple**
Penny pincher	**Penny Pincher**
Pete's sake	**Pete Sake**
Price you pay	**Price Yuhpaye**
Raising cane	**Ray Zencane**
Riffraff	**Rif Raff**
Read them and weep	**Rita Mehnweep**
Robbing the cradle	**Robin DeCraydull**
Rustle up some grub	**Russell Upsumgrubb**

Rude awakening	**Ruud Awakening**
Share and share alike	**Sharon Shairalike**
Shell of himself	**Shell Luvihmself**
Spade's a spade	**Spade Zaspayde**
Sticks and stones	**Stic Zenstones**
Stone cold	**Stone Cold**
Superdooper	**Sue Pirdooper**
Wall to wall	**Walt Tuwahl**
Whoopee do	**Whoopi Doo**
Why it behooves you	**Wyatt BeHoovsia**
Save your breath	**Xavier Breath**
You're killing me	**York Killinnmey**
You the man	**Yuda Mann**

Questions & Curiosities

ORIGIN OF NAME	NAME TO BE
How much are you charging?	**Alma Char'yuchargin**
How much is it?	**Alma Chisit**
Odd enough	**Audie Nuff**
Odd remarks	**Audrey Marx**
Odd reply	**Audrey Plye**
Odd response	**Audrey Sponce**
Odd result	**Audrey Zult**
Do we cheat them and how?	**Duey Cheatumenhow**
Heard a rumor	**Herta Rumor**
Hey would you blow me?	**Heywood Jablomee**
Hey would you mind?	**Heywood Jamind**
Who'd he knock up?	**Hootie Naukupp**
Who'd he suck up to?	**Hootie Succuptu**
Who'd he talk to?	**Hootie Toctu**
Who the fuck are you?	**Houda Fakarya**
Who'd have known?	**Houda Noan**
How'd he act?	**Howdy Act**

How'd he do?	**Howdy Doo**
How'd he do it?	**Howdy Duit**
How'd he get in?	**Howdy Giddin**
How'd he hit them?	**Howdy Hiddum**
How'd he shoot?	**Howdy Shoot**
Is a bell ringing?	**Isabell Ringing**
Is a door ajar?	**Isadore Adjarr**
Is a door open?	**Isadore Roapen**
Is a door shut?	**Isadore Schutt**
Is he dead?	**Izzy Dedd**
Is he done?	**Izzy Dunn**
Is he easy?	**Izzy Eazie**
Is he here?	**Izzy Heer**
Is he into it?	**Izzy Intuit**
Is he coming?	**Izzy Kumming**
Is he mad?	**Izzy Madd**
Is he ready?	**Izzy Ready**
Is he willing?	**Izzy Willing**
Did you ask permission?	**Jasper Mission**
Want some more?	**Juan Simohr**
Want to feel?	**Juana Feele**
Want to go?	**Juana Goe**
Want a job?	**Juana Jobb**
Want to come along?	**Juana Kummalong**
Want another one?	**Juana Notherwun**
Curiosity	**Keary Oscity**
Can I play?	**Ken Nieplay**
Can you dig it?	**Ken Yuhdiggit**
Imagine that	**Madge Inthat**
Maybe so	**Maye Beasoe**
Now do you believe me?	**Nadia BeLeivmee**
Now do you see me?	**Nadia Cecmcy**
Now do you get it?	**Nadia Giddit**

Need a break	Nita Braike
Need a lift	Nita Lift
No way	Noe Way
Hope he's okay	Opie Zokae
Pauly want a cracker?	Polly Wahnacrackir
Rumor has it	Rumour Hazzett
Rumors abound	Rumour Zahbound
Why'd he do it?	Whitey Duit
Why'd he quit?	Whitey Quit
Will his car start?	Willis Carstart
Will his dick fit?	Willis Dickphit
Will his wang work?	Willis Wangwork
Will my car start?	Wilma Carstart
Will my dick fit?	Wilma Dickphit
Is there another one?	Zeron Notherwun

Factual Statements

ORIGIN OF NAME	NAME TO BE
At least it's over	Adlee Stitsover
I'm on your side	Ahman Yoesighde
I'll explain it	Alex Plainitt
A net will catch him	Annette Uhlkachum
Are no more	Arno Moore
Been into it	Ben Nintuit
Been there	Ben Thair
Bumped into me	Bump Tintuhmee
Cold outside	Cole Doutside
Indeed he do	Dede Doo
Don't know nothing	Doan Noenutin
Door is ajar	Doris Adjarr
Door is shut	Doris Schutt
Door is open	Doris Soapin
He lies a lot	Eli Zahlott

Free to go	**Freida Goe**
Free to leave	**Frieda Leeve**
Gaines approval	**Gaines Approoval**
Guaranteed	**Garon Teed**
Glad it's over now	**Gladys Overnow**
Glad it's over with	**Gladys Overwith**
Heard about it	**Herta Boudit**
I'd agree	**Ida Gree**
I don't know nothing	**Ida Noenutin**
I disagree	**Ida Sugree**
I concede	**Ike Conceid**
I can see you	**Ike Conseayou**
I killed her	**Ike Killdurr**
I concur	**Ike Kuncurr**
I'm afraid	**Ima Fraid**
I'm a hoe	**Ima Hoe**
I'm a man	**Ima Mann**
I own a car	**Iona Carr**
I own a house	**Iona House**
I own them all	**Iona Maul**
I recall	**Ira Kaul**
I remember	**Ira Member**
I resisted	**Ira Zisstidd**
I've an idea	**Ivan Ideah**
I've been whacking off	**Ivan Yakonov**
Loud enough	**Lowden Nuff**
Low enough	**Lowen Nuff**
My loan's approved	**Malone Zuhprooved**
Me afraid	**Mia Fraid**
Many more	**Minnie Moore**
Never know that	**Nev Vernoothat**
Nor would I care	**Norwood Diekare**
Nor would it matter	**Norwood Dittmadder**

Power's off	**Powers Zoff**
Power's out	**Powers Zout**
Ran till he caught him	**Randa Leacawttum**
Scout's honor	**Scout Zahner**
See more clearly	**Seymour Clearly**
Standing room only	**Stan Dingroomoanly**
Some are into it	**Summer Rintuitt**
Tad small	**Tadd Small**
Tad too big	**Tadd Toobig**
Testimonial	**Tess DeMoaneayull**
Yet another one	**Yetta Notherwun**
Exactly	**Zack Lee**

Responding With Requests

ORIGIN OF NAME	NAME TO BE
I need another one	**Anita Notherwun**
I need a ride	**Anita Ride**
Odd Request	**Audrey Quest**
Bare in mind	**Baron Mind**
Be alert	**Bea Alert**
Bear down	**Bear Down**
Bear with me	**Bear Withmey**
Bud out	**Bud Dout**
Buzz off	**Buzz Zoff**
Calling out	**Caulen Nowt**
Don't dye	**Doan Dye**
Don't leave	**Doan Leeve**
Don't move	**Doan Move**
Don't quit	**Doan Quit**
Don't stop	**Doan Stop**
Fondle my sack	**Fawn Dullmasac**
Giddy up	**Giddy Yupp**
Let me go	**Lem Ego**

Let me down	**Lem Meedown**
Let's begin	**Les BeGinn**
Lead him in	**Lita Mihn**
Loosen up	**Lucen Nupp**
Nod your head	**Najeh Hedd**
Never mind	**Nev Ermind**
On your feet	**Onya Feet**
On your hands and knees	**Onya Hanzinease**
On your toes	**Onya Toes**
Park her right here	**Parker Ryddeer**
Pat my groin	**Pat McGroin**
Fill it up	**Phil Littupp**
Fill my crack in	**Phil McCracken**
Fill my crevasse	**Phil McKrevyss**
Fill some air time	**Phil Summairtime**
Roll over now	**Rolo Vernow**
Remain calm	**Romaine Calm**
Remain seated	**Romaine Seated**
Roll me over now	**Romeo Vernow**
See more samples	**Seymour Samples**
Sit down	**Sid Down**
Simon says	**Simon Sez**
Stay seated please	**Stacy Tiddpleaz**
Stand by me	**Stan Bymey**
Stand aside	**Stan DeSide**
Stand down	**Stan Down**
Stand up	**Stan Dupp**
Start again	**Starr Duhginn**
Take it away	**Tae Kiddaway**
Take it easy	**Tae Kiddeazy**
Tone down	**Tone Down**
Turn her over	**Turner Rover**
Wait and see	**Waite Encee**

Wait for me	**Waite Firmee**
Wait here	**Waite Heer**
Wait up	**Waite Upp**

THE THRIVING WORLD OF SPORTS

Equipment & Facilities

ORIGIN OF NAME	NAME TO BE
A netting	Annette Ting
Barbell	Barb Belle
Bevel knife	Bev Uhlnife
Bobsled	Bob Sled
Charity stripe	Charity Stripe
Clay court	Clay Court
Clay pigeon	Clay Pidgeon
Deuce coupe	Deuce Koop
Dodo scale	Dodo Scale
Dugout	Doug Gout
Face mask	Faye Smask
Fuzzy ball	Fuzzy Bahl
Helmut cam	Helmut Camm
Helmut strap	Helmut Strapp
Homer hanky	Homer Hanky
Indy car	Indy Carr
Jock strap	Jacque Strapp
Gymnasium	Jim Nasium
Gym shorts	Jim Shoarts
Line of scrimmage	Linus Scrimmage
Main entry	Maye Nentrie
Pace car	Pace Carr
Polly Pavilion	Polly Pavilyun
Race track	Ray Strack
Zamboni	Sam Boney
Ski boots	Skee Boots
Ski mask	Skee Mask
Ski slope	Skee Slope
Sky box	Sky Box

Slick approach	Slick Approche
Spring board	Spring Board
Test ball	Tess Bahl
Uniform	Una Form
Vent hole	Ven Tole
Weight hole	Waite Hole
Winston car	Winston Carr

Events

ORIGIN OF NAME	NAME TO BE
Bowling	Beau Ling
Boating	Beau Ting
Best ball	Bess Bahl
Charity event	Charity Event
Contest	Conn Test
Davis cup	Davis Cupp
Demolition	Dem Mohlishun
Diving	Di Ving
Fox hunt	Fox Hunt
Hurdling	Herta Ling
Hunting	Hunt Ting
Indy race	Indy Race
Gymnastics	Jim Nastiks
Marathon	Mare Rithonn
Marshall arts	Marshall Arts
Main event	Maye Nivent
Mini camp	Minnie Camp
Pep assembly	Pep Pahscembley
Pep rally	Pep Rallie
Rain delay	Rain DeLaye
Rained out	Rain Dout
Rain out	Ray Nowt
Racing	Ray Singh

Spring training	Spring Training
Stanley cup	Stanley Cupp
Cycling	Sy Cling
Tee time	Tee Tyme
Training camp	Tray Ningcamp
Taekwondo	Ty Kwondo
Winston cup	Winston Cupp

Fans, Coaching & Front Office Decisions

ORIGIN OF NAME	NAME TO BE
Ate him up	Aida Mupp
I'll race you	Al Rayshia
At least you tried	Alicia Tride
Band wagon	Ban Dwagon
Bowl well	Beau Well
Benching	Ben Ching
Besting	Bess Ting
Boo louder	Boo Louder
Boo losers	Boo Louzers
Cap room	Cap Rume
Chanting	Chan Ting
Die hard	Di Hard
Even you can win	Eve Venuekenwynn
Fair enough	Farrah Nuff
Fat chance	Fat Chance
Franchise	Fran Chise
Holding out	Holden Nowt
Idolize	Ida Lies
Coaching	Ko Ching
Motto	Maude Oh
Pad my stats	Padma Stats
Pep talk	Pep Talk
Renegotiate	Rena Goeshiate

Roster	**Ross Sturr**
Rowdy crowd	**Rowdy Kraud**
Salary cap	**Sal Recap**
Sentimental	**Senta Mental**
Slim chance	**Slim Chance**
Sterling performance	**Sterling Pirformints**
Teammate	**Tee Mayte**
Trade offer	**Tray Dawfurr**
Trading	**Tray Ding**
Trader	**Tray Durr**
Tough decision	**Tuff DeCision**
We'll race you	**Wil Rayshia**
Will to win	**Wilda Winn**
You'll lose	**Yuell Luze**
You'll win	**Yuell Winn**

Plays In Progress

ORIGIN OF NAME	NAME TO BE
Aiming high	**Aemon High**
Aiming low	**Aemon Lowe**
And he pops it up	**Andy Popsidupp**
And he scores	**Andy Scoars**
And he's in there	**Andy Zinthair**
And he's out	**Andy Zout**
Beaning	**Bea Ning**
Buzzer beater	**Buzz Urbeeter**
Castoff	**Cass Doff**
Catching	**Cat Ching**
Calling off	**Caulen Noff**
Count ball	**Count Bahl**
Fade away	**Faye DeWay**
Floater	**Flo Turr**
Forward progress	**Ford Prawgress**

Gaines ground	**Gaines Ground**
Gaines possession	**Gaines Pahseshun**
Gaines yardage	**Gaines Yardage**
Gaining	**Gay Ning**
Grand slam	**Grand Slam**
Hail Mary	**Hale Marry**
Head of steam	**Hedda Steam**
Lane maintenance	**Lane Maintinnince**
Lead off	**Lee Doff**
Leaner	**Lee Nurr**
Major error	**Major Airurr**
Major penalty	**Major Penulty**
Fill ball	**Phil Bahl**
Picked off	**Pic Doff**
Pick off	**Pic Oph**
Popped out	**Pop Dout**
Popped up	**Pop Dupp**
Pop out	**Pop Out**
Ranging	**Rain Jingh**
Ricochet	**Rick O'Shea**
Rolled away	**Roald DeWay**
Rolling strikes	**Roland Strikes**
Surge forward	**Serge Forword**
Slick move	**Slick Move**
Tip off	**Tip Oph**
Tip in	**Tip Pihn**

Individual Activities

ORIGIN OF NAME	NAME TO BE
A lane man	**Alaine Mann**
A net minder	**Annette Minedurr**
Bell sounds	**Belle Sounds**
Bronco rider	**Bronko Ryder**

Calisthenics	**Cal Listennex**
Cliff diver	**Cliff Diver**
Derby winner	**Derby Winner**
Fisherman	**Fischer Munn**
Guarding	**Garr Ding**
Hacked at it	**Hack Daddit**
Hurdle over it	**Herta Loaveritt**
Hurdler	**Herta Lurr**
High diver	**Hy Diver**
Lane man	**Lane Mann**
Leaping	**Lee Ping**
Lead a squad	**Lita Squad**
Marksman	**Mark Smun**
Marlon fishing	**Marlon Fishing**
Net a big one	**Netta Bigwun**
Net a fish	**Netta Fish**
Pearl diver	**Pearl Diver**
Rolled a ball	**Roald DeBahl**
Roll a ball	**Rolla Bahl**
Roll a strike	**Rolla Strike**
Shag flies	**Shag Flies**
Skip rope	**Skip Rope**
Sky diver	**Sky Diver**
Spike the ball	**Spike DeBahl**
Tee off	**Tee Oph**
Tee it up	**Tia Dupp**
Trainer	**Tray Nurr**
Victory lap	**Victor Relapp**

Commentary & Analysis

ORIGIN OF NAME	NAME TO BE
Arch enemy	**Arch Enemy**
Arch rival	**Arch Rival**

Are no losers	**Arno Louzers**
Bearing down	**Baron Down**
Blaze of glory	**Blaise O'Glory**
Blazing	**Blaise Zing**
Burned out	**Burn Dout**
Cliff hanger	**Cliff Hanger**
Day to celebrate	**Data Selibrate**
Dutch 200	**Dutch Touhundrid**
Facing	**Faye Singh**
Gage distance	**Gage Distance**
Gage speed	**Gage Speed**
Gage time	**Gage Tyme**
Gaines momentum	**Gaines Momentum**
Gaines an edge	**Gaines Zunedge**
Game on	**Gay Mawn**
Game over	**Gay Moaver**
Glory years	**Glory Years**
Golden opportunity	**Golden Noppirtunity**
Heady player	**Hedy Player**
Held an edge	**Helda Nedge**
Homer power	**Homer Power**
Hone his skills	**Honus Skills**
How he stands	**Howie Stanz**
Hundred over	**Hunter Dover**
Hundred under	**Hunter Dunder**
High score	**Hy Scoar**
Jacked up	**Jack Dupp**
June swoon	**June Swoon**
Just enough	**Justin Nuff**
Leading	**Lee Ding**
Leader	**Lee Durr**
Loosely guarded	**Lou Sleagardlhd**
Losing	**Lou Zing**

Low and outside	Lowen Outside
Lucky pairing	Lucky Perring
Margin for error	Marge Ginferrerer
Max power	Max Power
Momentum	Moe Mentum
All he can get	Ollie Kengitt
O and 2	Owen Tu
Fill frames	Phil Frames
Primo donna	Primo Donna
Real deal	Real Deal
Red hot	Red Hot
Regulation	Reg Yulaishunn
Rolled out	Roald Dout
Trailing	Tray Ling
Victory	Vic Torrey

SEARCHING FOR ANSWERS

Ailments

ORIGIN OF NAME	NAME TO BE
I'm on fire	Ahman Fire
Aching bones	Akin Bones
Aching pain	Akin Paine
Band aide	Ban Daide
Beat up	Bea Dupp
Benign	Bea Nine
Bee sting	Bea Sting
Beating	Bea Ting
Buckle under	Buck Cullunder
Cataract	Cat Tirract
Chapping	Chap Ping
Charlie horse	Charlie Hoarse
Chip her tooth	Chipper Tooth
Dizziness	Dizzy Ness
Dizzy spells	Dizzy Spels
Hurt a lot	Herta Lott
Hurt a little	Herta Lyttle
Hung over	Hung Over
I've an awful itch	Ivan Noffulitch
Kiel Dover	Keil Dover
Kiel over	Keil Loaver
Languishing	Lang Gwishing
Malnourished	Mal Nirrisht
Memory laps	Memory Lapse
Mercury poisoning	Mercury Poisning
Moaning	Moe Ning
Nicked up	Nick Dupp
Oh this hurts	Otis Hurtz
Pain and sorrow	Payne Ensaro

Pain and suffering	**Payne Ensuffrin**
Reoccurring	**Rhea Kurring**
Snake bite	**Snake Byte**
Sore enough	**Soren Nuff**
Sore and painful	**Soren Painful**
Sore and swelling	**Soren Swelling**
Spider bite	**Spider Byte**
Spring fever	**Spring Fever**
Stigmatism	**Stig Muttizam**
Thorough beating	**Thurrell Beating**
Torn apart	**Tor Nipart**
Vega bond	**Vega Bond**
Whip lash	**Whip Lash**
Will burn and peel	**Wilbur Nenpeal**
Winced in pain	**Winston Paine**

Disease, Phobias & Warnings

ORIGIN OF NAME	NAME TO BE
A man to be reckoned with	**Amanda BeReckondwith**
A man to fear	**Amanda Fear**
Anorexia	**Anna Rexia**
Arch villain	**Arch Villain**
Barbaric	**Barb Airrick**
Barbarian	**Barb Barion**
Bulimia	**Bill Leamiah**
Carcinoma	**Carson Ohma**
Colon cancer	**Colen Kansurr**
Danger	**Dain Jurr**
Derelicts	**Darryl Licks**
Dialysis	**Di Alyssis**
Epidemic	**Eppa Demmick**
Epilepsy	**Eppa Lepsie**
Evil empire	**Eve Uhlempire**

Evaporate	Eve Vaporate
Frantic lee	Fran Tiklee
Gale warning	Gail Warning
Halitosis	Hal Latosis
Jolting	Joel Ting
Laryngitis	Laron Jidas
Leukemia	Lou Keemiah
Lunatic	Luna Tick
Magnitude	Mag Nittude
May Day	Maye Daye
Melanoma	Mel LaNoma
Melancholy	Mel Lynncauley
Petrify	Petra Fye
Ransom note	Ransom Note
Raider	Ray Durr
Raging	Ray Jingh
Salmonella	Sal Manilla
Scarlet fever	Scarlett Fever
Shy away	Shia Way
Snake bit	Snake Bitt
Stand off	Stan Doff
Storm chasers	Storm Chaisers
Storm warning	Storm Warning
Psychosis	Sy Coasis
Psychotic	Sy Cottick
Terrify	Terra Fye
Timber	Tim Burr

Law & Order

ORIGIN OF NAME	NAME TO BE
Alimony	Al Amoany
Barely legal	Bear LeLegal
Bill collector	Bill Collecktor
Book her and lock her up	Booker Enlockerupp
Book her for fraud	Booker Firfraud
Case files	Case Files
Case history	Case History
Calling all cars	Caulen Nawlcarrs
Cease her belongings	Ceasar Belongings
Seal your fate	Celia Faite
Chase cars	Chase Karrs
Chasing	Chase Singh
Caught and convicted	Cotton Cunvicted
Duly served	Dooley Servd
Federal agent	Federal Agent
Federal building	Federal Billding
Federal court	Federal Court
Federal law	Federal Law
Federal offense	Federal O'Phence
Federal Penn	Federal Penn
Guillotine	Gil Lahteen
Guilty verdict	Gil Teaverdict
Gestapo	Gus Toppo
Haul his ass away	Hollis Sascaway
Haul his ass to jail	Hollis Sastajale
Hung jury	Hung Jury
Judgmental	Judge Mental
Justice for all	Justice Furrahl
Justice prevails	Justice Prevails
Casing	Kay Singh
Late and disciplined	Layton Dissaplind

Legality	**Lee Gallity**
Legal aide	**Lee Gullade**
Legal limit	**Lee Gullimit**
Lean them up	**Lena Mupp**
Loophole	**Lupe Hoal**
Magistrate	**Madge Istraite**
Marshall law	**Marshall Law**
Merritt system	**Merritt System**
Miranda act	**Miranda Act**
Miranda rights	**Miranda Wrights**
Noting	**Noe Ting**
Notary public	**Nota Republik**
Paddy wagon	**Patty Wagon**
Pending	**Penn Ding**
Police	**Poe Lease**
Polygraph	**Polly Graph**
Retrospect	**Rhett Troespect**
Retribution	**Rhett Truhbiewshun**
Read him his rights	**Rita Mizwrights**
Redirect	**Rita Recht**
Right or wrong	**Ryder Rong**
Citation	**Sy Tation**
Tainted evidence	**Tain Tiddevidence**
Tainting	**Tain Ting**
Theoretically	**Theo Rhetiklee**
Thorough search	**Thurrell Surch**
Tipped off	**Tip Doff**
Trace tracks	**Trace Tracks**
Trade off	**Tray Doff**
Trace evidence	**Tray Sehvidence**
Vindicate	**Vin Dicate**
Vito power	**Vito Power**
Will reconvene	**Wilrey Kenvean**

Medical Practice

ORIGIN OF NAME	NAME TO BE
I'll examine her	Alex Zamuner
Angioplasty	Angie O'Plastee
Angiosperm	Angie O'Sperm
I feel your heartbeat	Aphelia Hartbeat
Bend over	Ben Dover
Cat scan	Cat Scann
Call in sick	Caulen Syk
Coroner	Cora Nurr
Dixie cup	Dixie Cupp
Dyer need	Dyer Knead
Urinalysis	Eura Nalyssis
Faring well	Faron Well
Face lift	Faye Slift
Fester	Fes Turr
Fermentation	Furman Tation
Gerontology	Ger Entollgy
Genealogy	Jeannie Olligy
Geriatrics	Jerry Attrix
Just inhale	Justin Hale
Chemistry	Kem Mistry
List her vitals	Lister Vitals
Malpractice	Mal Practice
Metamorphosis	Meta Morphis
Mortuary	Mort Chuarry
Mortician	Mort Tission
Normality	Norm Alitty
Orally administered	Oralee Administurd
Oral hygiene	Orel Hygeen
Pace maker	Pace Maker
Pop a boil	Papa Boyle
Pop a pimple	Papa Pimpl

Past her physical	**Paster Fizzickle**
Painless	**Payne Lis**
Periodontal	**Perry O'Dontel**
Pediatrics	**Petey Attrix**
Pediatrician	**Petey Yuhtrischun**
Pierced ear	**Pierce Deer**
Piercing	**Pierce Singh**
Cerebellum	**Sara Bellum**
Cesarean	**Sue Serrion**
Testosterone	**Tess Tosterone**
Thermometer	**Thurm Aumitter**
Treating	**Tree Ting**
Vernacular	**Vern Ackular**
Vitally	**Vida Lee**

IT'S A SAD STATE OF AFFAIRS

Criminal Activity

ORIGIN OF NAME	NAME TO BE
Baby raper	Babe BeRaiper
Beat her	Bea Turr
Belting	Belle Ting
Breeching	Brea Ching
Bust her chops	Buster Chopps
Bust her out	Buster Out
Cloning	Cloe Ning
Conned again	Conn Duhginn
Con man	Conn Mann
Con artist	Conn Nardist
Con her into it	Connor Rintuitt
Fess up	Fes Supp
Grand larceny	Grand Larcenie
Grand scheme	Grand Sceam
Gun her down	Gunnar Down
Hand it over	Hana Dover
Hands up	Hans Upp
Held it up	Helda Dupp
Heard another one	Herta Notherwun
Her disguise	Herta Skies
Hindering	Hind Durring
Huckster	Huck Sturr
Hint him down	Hunt Ihmdown
Hunt her down	Hunter Down
Heisting	Hy Sting
Jay walker	Jay Walker
Jewel thief	Jewel Theaf
Kidnapper	Kidd Napper
Kiddy porn	Kitty Porn

Lady killer	**Lady Killer**
Leeching	**Lee Ching**
Light him on fire	**Lida Monfire**
Loitering	**Lloyd Durring**
Laundering	**Lon Durring**
Looting	**Lou Ting**
Loiter	**Loy Durr**
Matricide	**Matt Tricide**
Pick pocket	**Pic Pocket**
Poaching	**Poe Ching**
Rape and sodomy	**Ray Pensawdumy**
Raping	**Ray Ping**
Rapist	**Ray Pisst**
Wrecks cars	**Rex Karrs**
Rob banks	**Rob Banks**
Robbed her	**Rob Durr**
Ruthless	**Ruth Lis**
She'll attack it	**Sheila Tackett**
Stick up	**Stic Cupp**
Stalk her daily	**Stockard Daly**
Tampering	**Tam Purring**
Torture	**Tor Churr**
Traitor	**Tray Turr**
Vandalize	**Van DeLies**
Victimize	**Vic DeMize**
Will burn it up	**Wilbur Nidupp**
Will burn it down	**Wilbur Nitdown**

Death, Disaster & Tragedy

ORIGIN OF NAME	**NAME TO BE**
Atom splits	**Adam Splitz**
Buried alive	**Barry Delighve**
Buried under	**Barry Dunder**

Burned up	**Burn Dupp**
Burning	**Burn Ning**
Capsize	**Cap Sighs**
Castrate	**Cass Strait**
Castration	**Cass Traishun**
Catastrophic	**Cat Estrawfick**
Crash and burn	**Crash Enburn**
Crash landing	**Crash Landing**
Day to lament	**Data LaMent**
Day to mourn	**Data Mourne**
Decompose	**Deacon Poase**
Died out	**Di Dout**
Die young	**Di Young**
Dug my grave	**Doug McGrave**
Epicenter	**Eppa Center**
Fatality	**Faye Talitty**
Forest fire	**Forrest Fire**
Gassed and burned	**Gaston Burnd**
Harming each other	**Harmon Neichuther**
Held a hostage	**Helda Hostage**
Mal nutrition	**Mal Nutrician**
Man eater	**Manny Turr**
Mercy killing	**Mercy Killing**
Mourn a dead man	**Morna Deadman**
Mortify	**Morta Fye**
Mortally	**Morta Lee**
More to lose	**Morta Luze**
Hope he doesn't die	**Opie Duzzendie**
Raiding	**Ray Ding**
Starvation	**Starr Vation**
Starving	**Starr Ving**
Suicide	**Sue Iscide**
Thirst and hunger	**Thurston Hungar**

Trembles	**Trem Bolles**
Tremulous	**Trem Ulyss**
Unabomber	**Una Bommer**

Hardships & Difficulties

ORIGIN OF NAME	NAME TO BE
Bummed out	**Bum Dout**
Bum steer	**Bum Steer**
Burn up	**Burn Nupp**
Castaway	**Cass Tahway**
Crashed again	**Crash Duhginn**
Crash into it	**Crash Intuitt**
Day to forget	**Data Firgitt**
Denting	**Den Ting**
Denting cars	**Denton Karrs**
Dicked over	**Dick Dover**
Dicked around	**Dick Durroun**
Dire strait	**Dyer Strait**
Flipped over	**Flip Dover**
Flipping	**Flip Ping**
Gaping	**Gay Ping**
Hapless	**Hap Lis**
Hard enough	**Hardie Nuff**
Hopeless	**Hope Lis**
Hostility	**Hoss Stillity**
Hostile	**Hoss Tile**
Jack knife	**Jack Nife**
Coping	**Ko Ping**
Low esteem	**Lois Esteam**
Major pain	**Major Paine**
Moping	**Moe Ping**
No avail	**Noah Vale**
Pouting	**Pau Ting**

ORIGIN OF NAME	NAME TO BE
Ranting	**Rand Ting**
Wrecks homes	**Rex Holmes**
Tipped over	**Tip Dover**
Tip her over	**Tipper Rover**
Tough time	**Tuff Tyme**
Tied up	**Ty Dupp**
Venting	**Ven Ting**
Whipped again	**Whip Duhginn**
You're evicted	**Yori Victidd**

Weaponry & World At War

ORIGIN OF NAME	NAME TO BE
Atom bomb	**Adam Baum**
Android	**Ann Droid**
Aerial attack	**Arial LaTack**
Aerial assault	**Arial Lussault**
Bandelier	**Ban DeLier**
Barbed wire	**Barb Dwyer**
Bow and arrow	**Beau Wynnarrow**
Birth of a nation	**Bertha Venation**
B.B. gun	**Bibi Gunn**
Billy club	**Billy Club**
Brick bat	**Brick Batt**
British troops	**Britt Ishtroops**
Buck knife	**Buck Nife**
Cap gun	**Cap Gunn**
Sharp instrument	**Char Pihnstrumint**
Christian soldier	**Christian Soldier**
Claymore	**Clay Moore**
Camouflage	**Com O'Flojg**
Derringer	**Darren Jurr**
D Day	**Dee Daye**
Dynamite	**Dyna Myte**

Emil nitraite	Emil Nytraite
Evasion	Eve Asian
Fleet of ships	Fleta Shipps
Fox hole	Fox Hoal
Guard duty	Garr Dooty
Geneva convention	Geneva Cuhnvenshun
Guided missile	Guy Didmissul
Held a gun	Helda Gunn
Hide out	Hy Dout
Chemical	Kem Mickel
Lance Corporal	Lance Corporal
Lead them in to battle	Lita Mihndabaddle
Launching	Lon Ching
Lieutenant	Lou Tenant
Neo Nazi	Neo Natzee
Neutralize	Newt Trulize
Parachute	Paris Shoot
Pepper spray	Pepper Spray
Periscope	Per Ruhscope
Pop gun	Pop Gunn
Radar	Ray Darr
Ray gun	Ray Gunn
Red leader	Red Leeder
Rip cord	Rip Kord
Roman empire	Roman Empire
Shell shock	Shell Shock
Spring loaded	Spring Loaded
Storm trooper	Storm Trooper
Cyborg	Sy Borg
Tanker	Tank Kerr
Toy gun	Toi Gunn
Tomahawk	Tom O'Hawk
Tommy gun	Tommy Gunn

Torching	**Tor Ching**
Torpedo	**Tor Peido**
Vanguard	**Van Gaard**
War and peace	**Warren Peece**

GROWING UP AND THEN SOME

Family Matters & Parental Guidance

ORIGIN OF NAME	NAME TO BE
I'll be quiet	Albie Quiet
Bare essentials	Bear Riscentials
Best behavior	Bess BeHavior
Best man	Bess Mann
Constant supervision	Constance Supervision
Don't you dare	Doan Judare
Don't touch it	Doan Tuchit
Flower child	Flower Child
Foster child	Foster Child
Foster homes	Foster Holmes
Foster care	Foster Kair
Foster parent	Foster Parent
Gene pool	Gene Poole
Grand child	Grand Child
Grand father	Grand Fawther
Grand mother	Grand Mother
Hands off	Hans Zoff
Generosity	Jenn Norrositty
Late and pregnant	Layton Pregnant
Leave it alone	Lee Vittalone
Marry and divorce	Marion Divorce
Oh be good	Obie Goode
Oh behave	Obie Haive
Oh be nice	Obie Nice
Oh be quiet	Obie Quiet
Oh be still	Obie Still
Pampering	Pam Purring
Past her bedtime	Paster Bedtime
Picked at it	Pic Daddit

Piper down	**Piper Down**
Raising	**Ray Zing**
Rise and shine	**Rhys Zenshine**
Shame on you	**Shea Monyu**
Shape up	**Shea Pupp**
Sit up	**Sid Dupp**
Simmer down	**Sim Mirrdown**
Stand by your man	**Stan Buyerrmann**
Stand still	**Stan Still**
Stand straight	**Stan Strait**
Sweet as can be	**Swede Deskenbee**
Sweetie pie	**Swede Eaypie**
Silence	**Sy Lence**
Tip toe	**Tip Towe**
Toddler	**Todd Lurr**
Tom boy	**Tom Buoy**
Tuck her in	**Tucker Inn**
Wait right here	**Waite Ryddeer**

Household Chores & Labor

ORIGIN OF NAME	NAME TO BE
Build up	**Bill Dupp**
Cat box	**Cat Box**
Daily chores	**Dailey Chores**
Draining	**Drae Ning**
Do we have to?	**Duey Hafta**
Dust and debris	**Dustin DuBree**
Dusty table	**Dusty Table**
Herbicide	**Herb Biscide**
Kitty litter	**Kitty Litter**
Laundromat	**Lon Drummatt**
Lawn mower	**Lon Mower**
Made your bed	**Major Bedd**

Manuel labor	**Manuel Labor**
Mows lawns	**Mose Lawns**
Mows his grass	**Moses Grass**
Mows his own yard	**Moses Ownyard**
Need a hand?	**Nita Hand**
Pooper scooper	**Pooh Pirscooper**
Pressed and clean	**Preston Clean**
Pressed and folded	**Preston Folded**
Pressed in place	**Preston Place**
Raking leaves	**Ray Kenleeves**
Roof is leaking	**Rufus Leaking**
Scot towel	**Scott Towell**
Spin Cycle	**Spin Cycle**
Squeaky clean	**Squeaky Clean**
Terrycloth	**Terry Cloth**
Walk her dog	**Walker Dawg**

Vacations, Holidays & Happy Times

ORIGIN OF NAME	NAME TO BE
Anti social	**Antti Soashall**
Birth of the blues	**Bertha DeBlews**
Best of all	**Bess Duvall**
Bossa Nova	**Boss Senova**
Dine out	**Di Nowt**
Glorious	**Glory Yuss**
Golden years	**Golden Years**
Halleluiah	**Halle Lewyah**
Hap hazard	**Hap Hazzard**
Happy holiday	**Happy Holiday**
Hope it's good	**Hope Pittsgoode**
He aint going no where	**Ian Gowenowaire**
Idly	**Ida Lee**
Call your mother	**Kolya Mother**

Leasing	**Lee Singh**
Leave on Friday	**Lee VonFriday**
Leave on time	**Lee VonTyme**
Mardi gras	**Marty Grah**
Mary Christmas	**Mary Crismuss**
Mary holiday	**Mary Holiday**
Made up	**Maye Dupp**
Napping	**Nap Ping**
Nap time	**Nap Tyme**
Roam around	**Roma Rown**
Roaming around	**Roman Rown**
Rendezvous	**Ron DaVue**
Spring break	**Spring Braike**
Spring vacation	**Spring Vacation**
Summer vacation	**Summer Vacation**
Tanning booth	**Tan Ningboothe**
Tom-tom	**Tom Tom**
Tuesday morning	**Tuesday Mourning**
Wednesday night	**Wednesday Knight**
Yuletide	**Yuell Tide**

SCHOOLING IS STILL THE BEST OPTION

Education & Learning

ORIGIN OF NAME	NAME TO BE
Our man don't know nothing	Armando Noenuthin
Art major	Art Major
Art school	Art Skool
Case he forgot	Casey Forgawt
Case he missed it	Casy Misditt
Chap book	Chap Book
Clerical	Claire Rickull
Clarify	Clara Fye
Date of absence	Data Vabscents
Dean ship	Dean Shipp
Don't be stupid	Doby Stupid
Doctrination	Dock Trinnism
Dawned on me	Don Dahnmey
Education	Ed Ewcashion
Elementary	Ella Mentry
Even I can win	Eve Venighcanwynn
Fair analogy	Farrah Nalogy
Failing	Faye Ling
Grading papers	Gradon Paypers
Grant and aide	Grant Inade
Hall monitor	Hall Monitor
Honor roll	Honor Rohle
How he does it	Howie Duzzit
Junior college	Junior College
Junior high	Junior High
Matching	Matt Ching
Meritorious	Merritt Orrious
Know enough	Noah Nuff
Note of absence	Nota Vabscents
Orientation	Orien Tation

Philosophical	**Phyliss Sophigull**
Rand to school	**Randa Skool**
Real smart	**Real Smart**
Rediscover	**Rita Scuvver**
Rusticate	**Russ Ticate**
Semicolon	**Semi Coalen**
Similarity	**Sim Mullaritty**
Skip school	**Skip Skool**
Student teacher	**Stu Denteacher**
Stupendous	**Stu Pendace**
Stupidity	**Stu Piditty**
Summer school	**Summer Skool**
Teaching	**Tee Ching**
Teacher	**Tee Churr**
Test paper	**Tess Payper**
Test score	**Tess Scoar**
Testing	**Tess Ting**
Tester	**Tess Turr**
Why it works	**Wyatt Works**
You don't know nothing	**Yuda Noenuthin**

Acting Responsibly

ORIGIN OF NAME	**NAME TO BE**
Be good	**Bea Goode**
Behave	**Bea Haive**
Be nice	**Bea Nice**
Be quiet	**Bea Quiet**
Be still	**Bea Still**
Be straight	**Bea Strait**
Calling in	**Caulen Ninn**
Don't do it	**Doan Duit**
Don't forget	**Doan Firgett**
Don't shoot	**Doan Shoot**
Don't be late	**Doby Late**

Freed another one	**Freida Notherwun**
Gargling	**Garr Gling**
Hair removal	**Harry Mouval**
Humility	**High Millitty**
Humane	**Hugh Maine**
High fidelity	**Hy Fidelitty**
Live right	**Liv Wright**
Loud and clear	**Lowden Clear**
Paid your bills	**Paige Jurrbills**
Paid your debt	**Paige Jurrdett**
Thoroughly	**Thurrell Lee**
Treat him fairly	**Treat Himfairly**
Treat them with respect	**Treat Tumwithrespekt**
Vitamin	**Vida Mihn**
Invite them over	**Vida Moaver**

Reading, Writing & Arithmetic

ORIGIN OF NAME	NAME TO BE
ABC's	**Abe BeCeeze**
Add them up	**Adam Mupp**
A to Z	**Aida Zee**
Alphabetical	**Alpha Bedickel**
Alphabetize	**Alpha BeTize**
Calculate	**Cal Kulate**
Calibrate	**Cal LeBrate**
Carry over	**Carrie Over**
Colin backslash	**Colen Backslash**
Count backward	**Count Backword**
Count digits	**Count Digits**
Counting	**Count Ting**
Dewey decimal	**Ducy Desimull**
Error in spelling	**Erin Spelling**
Estimate	**Esta Mayte**

Heard a story	**Herta Storrie**
Kelly Bluebook	**Kelly Bluebook**
Less digits	**Les Digits**
Page two	**Paige Tu**
Page turner	**Paige Turner**
Pamphlet	**Pam Flitt**
Pencil and pen	**Penn Sullinpenn**
Read books	**Red Books**
Read into it	**Red Intuit**
Read books	**Reed Books**
Read into it	**Reed Intuit**
Read a book	**Rhetta Book**
Read about it	**Rhetta Boudit**
Read it off	**Rhetta Doff**
Read it over	**Rhetta Dover**
Wrote a book	**Rhoda Book**
Wrote about it	**Rhoda Boudit**
Wrote it over	**Rhoda Dover**
Wrote a story	**Rhoda Storrie**
Read a book	**Rita Book**
Read about it	**Rita Boudit**
Read it off	**Rita Doff**
Read it out loud	**Rita Doubtloud**
Read it over	**Rita Dover**
Read it again	**Rita Duhginn**
Read a story	**Rita Storrie**
Roman numeral	**Roman Noomral**
Tabulate	**Tab Ulate**
Text book	**Tex Book**
Unilateral	**Una Lateral**

ENTERTAINMENT

Games, Cards & Wagers

ORIGIN OF NAME	NAME TO BE
Ace high	Ace High
Ace kicker	Ace Kicker
Ace in the hole	Ace Sindahoal
Acie deucie	Acie Deucie
Anti up	Antti Yupp
Atari games	Atari Gaimes
Bets enough	Betsy Nuff
Bingo	Bing Goe
Cash his chips in	Cassius Chipsinn
Chancing	Chan Singh
Chances are	Chance Sizzarr
Dealing	Dee Ling
Dealt a flush	Delta Flush
Dealt a hand	Delta Hand
Face up	Faye Supp
Gin rummy	Gin Rummy
Hedge bets	Hedge Betts
Held a hand	Helda Hand
High hand	Hy Hand
High stakes	Hy Stakes
Jack pot	Jack Pot
Joy stick	Joy Stic
Lowest bidder	Lois Bidder
Lucky day	Lucky Daye
Making bets	Megan Betts
Pat hand	Pat Hand
Pegged out	Peg Dout
Penny anti	Penny Antti
Penny slot	Penny Slot

Raise and re-raise	Ray Zenreraise
Raise it up	Ray Ziddupp
Rolled up	Roald Dupp
Robbed again	Rob Duhginn
Royal flush	Royal Flush
Solitaire	Sol Littair
Spade flush	Spade Flush
Spin freely	Spin Freely
Wait your turn	Waite Churturn

Hobbies, Toys & Recreation

ORIGIN OF NAME	NAME TO BE
April fools	April Fools
Art collector	Art Collektor
Arts and crafts	Art Sencrafts
Art supplies	Art Supplies
Babe watcher	Babe Watcher
Banter	Ban Turr
Barbie doll	Barbie Dahl
Bear trap	Bear Trapp
Birdie call	Birdie Kaul
Camping	Cam Ping
Carousel	Cara Cell
Cat call	Cat Kaul
Chase me down	Chase Meedown
Chris cross	Chris Cross
Dancing	Dan Singh
Dot-to-dot	Dot Tedott
Draws and doodles	Drazen Doodles
Drew pictures	Drew Pictures
Drew straws	Drew Strahs
Dutch treat	Dutch Treat
Emulate	Em Ulate

Ferris wheel	**Ferris Wheel**
Fox trot	**Fox Trot**
Fuzzy photo	**Fuzzy Photo**
Gazing	**Gay Zing**
High horse	**Hy Hoarse**
Joker	**Joe Kerr**
Joking	**Joe King**
Kayak	**Ki Yak**
Lincoln log	**Lincoln Lawg**
Lionel train	**Lionel Train**
Merry-go-round	**Mary Goerown**
Modulate	**Maude DeFighe**
Making	**Maye King**
Pasting	**Pace Ting**
Painting	**Payne Ting**
Poster	**Poe Sturr**
Pokey man	**Pokey Mawn**
Reassemble	**Rhea Semmbull**
Ring go round	**Ringo Rown**
Roman candle	**Roman Candle**
Simulate	**Sim Ulate**
Spin the bottle	**Spin DeBoddle**
Start over	**Starr Dover**
Stick figure	**Stic Figure**
Sticker	**Stic Kerr**
Tambourine	**Tam Boreine**
Teddy bear	**Teddy Bear**
Teeter totter	**Tee Tirtodder**
Toy box	**Toi Box**
Toy store	**Toi Storr**
Tom foolery	**Tom Foolery**
Tonka toy	**Tonka Toye**
Tonka trucks	**Tonka Trucks**

ORIGIN OF NAME	NAME TO BE
Training wheels	Tray Ningwheels
Tracing	Tray Singh
Wading	Wade Ding
Wading pool	Wade Ingpool
Whoopi cushion	Whoopi Cushun

Professional Entertainers & Worthy Performances

ORIGIN OF NAME	NAME TO BE
Art gallery	Art Gallery
Articulate	Art Ticulate
Art works	Art Works
Artistry	Artis Tree
Band leader	Ban Leeder
Band member	Ban Member
Band stand	Ban Stand
B Minor	Bea Miner
Best actor	Bess Tactor
Burlesque	Burl Lesque
Cameo	Cammie Oh
Captivate	Cap Tivate
Caroling	Carol Ling
Karaoke	Carrie Okie
Casting	Cass Ting
Clarinet	Clara Nett
Choreographer	Corey Augrapher
Choreograph	Corey O'Graffe
Curtain call	Curt Encall
Debonair	Deb Bonaire
D Minor	Dee Miner
Demonstrate	Dem Instraite
Dynamic	Di Namick
Duly honored	Dooley Honord
Emmy award	Emmy Award

Emmy winner	**Emmy Winner**
Eulogy	**Eula Gee**
Unison	**Eunice Sun**
Go-go dancer	**Gogo Dancer**
Go-go girl	**Gogo Gurhl**
Golden globe	**Golden Globe**
Grammy award	**Grammy Award**
Grammy winner	**Grammy Winner**
Grand Ole Opry	**Grand Ohlawpry**
Grand piano	**Grand Piano**
Harmonize	**Harmon Isze**
Harmony vocals	**Harmon Neavocals**
High wire	**Hy Wire**
Just an act	**Justin Act**
Magical	**Madge Ickel**
Magic trick	**Madge Icktrick**
Melody vocals	**Melody Vocals**
Microphone	**Mike Raphone**
Oscar nominee	**Oscar Nawminee**
Oscar winner	**Oscar Winner**
Pandemonium	**Panda Moanium**
Philharmonic	**Phil Harmonic**
Raving	**Ray Ving**
Reappears	**Rhea Peers**
Rendition	**Rhen Dishen**
Rock on	**Rock Awn**
Serenade	**Sara Nade**
Slight of hand	**Sly Tuhvhand**
Stand alone	**Stan DeLoan**
Stand out	**Stan Dout**
Star struck	**Starr Struk**
Superior	**Sue Peerior**
Tony award	**Tony Award**

Ventriloquist	Van Triloquist
Warner brothers	Warner Bruthers
World renowned	World Renownd
Yodeling	Yoda Ling
Yodeler	Yoda Lurr

WHAT A FASCINATING PLACE THIS IS

Landmarks & Traveling The World

ORIGIN OF NAME	NAME TO BE
Alabama	Al LaBamma
Archeology	Arky Olligy
Artifacts	Art Tifacts
Bay front	Bae Front
Bay shore	Bae Shore
Bantu	Ban Tu
Baron desert	Baron Desert
Blazing trails	Blaise Zentrails
British isles	Britt Ischisles
Carolina	Carol Lighna
Clod hopper	Claude Hopper
Coit tower	Coit Tower
Dakota territory	Dakota Territory
Delaware	Della Ware
Diamond mine	Diamond Mine
Illinois	Ellen Noy
Franklin mint	Franklin Mint
Grand Canyon	Grand Canyun
Hill to climb	Hilda Climb
Hacienda	Hoss Seyenda
Idaho	Ida Hoe
Indiana	Indy Anna
Kentucky	Ken Tucky
Lake front	Lake Front
Lake shore	Lake Shore
Land and sky	Landon Skie
Land and water	Landon Water
Lincoln memorial	Lincoln Memorial
Live on a hill	Livan Ahill

Louisiana	**Louise Zianna**
Mason Dixon	**Mason Dixon**
Marine waters	**Maureen Watters**
Minnesota	**Minna Sota**
Muddy waters	**Muddy Watters**
River banks	**River Banks**
River front	**River Front**
Rocks and rubble	**Roxanne Rubble**
Salt waters	**Salt Watters**
Sandy beach	**Sandy Beach**
Terra Firma	**Terra Firma**
Territory	**Terra Torrey**
Valley	**Val Lee**
Valley floor	**Vallie Floor**
Windy city	**Wendy Sittee**
West end	**Wes Tend**
Western world	**Wes Turnworld**
West Virginia	**Wes Virginia**

Mother Nature & The Weather

ORIGIN OF NAME	NAME TO BE
Amber waves	**Amber Waives**
April showers	**April Showers**
August heat	**August Heat**
Augustly	**August Lee**
Autumn days	**Autumn Daise**
Autumn night	**Autumn Knight**
Autumn leaves	**Autumn Leeves**
Autumn skies	**Autumn Skies**
Blue skies	**Blue Skize**
Breezing	**Brea Zing**
Crystal clear	**Crystal Clear**
Crystallize	**Crystal Isze**

Day to night	**Data Knight**
Donnybrook	**Donnie Brooke**
Early morning	**Early Mourning**
Gale storm	**Gail Storm**
Gale winds	**Gail Winns**
Gray skies	**Grace Skize**
Gusting	**Gus Ting**
Gust of wind	**Gus Tuhvwind**
Guster	**Gus Turr**
Hail stone	**Hale Stone**
Hail storm	**Hale Storm**
Highly	**Hy Lee**
High skies	**Hy Skize**
Ice sickle	**Ice Sickel**
Luke warm	**Luke Warm**
Marianna trench	**Marianna Trench**
Mercury rising	**Mercury Rising**
Misty morning	**Misty Mourning**
Quintessence	**Quinn Tessance**
Rain storm	**Rain Storm**
Rain or shine	**Rainer Shine**
Rainy days	**Rainey Daise**
Rainy night	**Rainey Knight**
Rainy skies	**Rainey Skize**
Raining	**Ray Ning**
Shading	**Shea Ding**
Sky blue	**Sky Bleu**
Sky so blue	**Sky Soeblue**
Skies above	**Sky Zahbuv**
Skies are blue	**Sky Zahrblue**
Sunny day	**Sonny Daye**
Sunny skies	**Sonny Skize**
Spring day	**Spring Daye**

Storm front	**Storm Front**
Storm windows	**Storm Windows**
Stormy night	**Stormy Knight**
Stormy skies	**Stormy Skize**
Stormy weather	**Stormy Weather**
Summer days	**Summer Daise**
Summer night	**Summer Knight**
Summer sky	**Summer Skie**
Cyclone	**Sy Clone**
Typhoon	**Ty Phune**
Windy days	**Wendy Daise**
Windy skies	**Wendy Skize**
Wilderness	**Wil Durness**

Outer Limits & The Super Natural

ORIGIN OF NAME	**NAME TO BE**
Beam up	**Bea Mupp**
Celestial	**Celeste Cheall**
Charlie's angels	**Charlie Zaingels**
Clairvoyant	**Claire Voyant**
Crystal ball	**Crystal Bahl**
Daunting	**Don Ting**
Eloquent	**Ella Quint**
Heaven on earth	**Evan Awnearth**
Heavenly days	**Evan Leadaze**
Heavenly angel	**Evan LeAngel**
Heavenly	**Evan Lee**
Heavenly skies	**Even Leaskies**
Fade out	**Faye Dout**
Guardian angel	**Garr D'Enaingel**
Grant a wish	**Grant Tuhwish**
Gypsy woman	**Gypsy Woman**
Horoscope	**Horace Scope**

Levitate	Lev Itate
Milky way	Mel Keeway
Meditating	Meta Tating
Miles apart	Miles Zehpart
Pearly gates	Pearlie Gates
Rise above it	Rhys Zuhbbuvitt
Rose above it all	Rosa Buhvidahl
Sell my soul	Selma Sole
Star gate	Starr Gate
Star gazer	Starr Gazer
Star light	Starr Lite
Star system	Starr System
Superstition	Sue Purstition
Suiting	Sue Ting
Sighting	Sy Ting
Violet rays	Violet Raze
Vividly	Viv Iddly

POTENTIALLY TURNING PROFITS

Advertising & Business

ORIGIN OF NAME	NAME TO BE
Art critic	Art Krittic
Avis cars	Avis Karrs
Avis rents	Avis Wrents
Banner	Ban Nurr
Best offer	Bess Toffer
Best western	Bess Western
Bill board	Bill Board
Cast your ballot	Cass Churballot
Cat house	Cat House
Closing	Cloe Zing
Close out	Cloe Zout
Closing up	Cloe Zynupp
Count the money	Count DeMoney
Courtesy call	Curtis Seacall
Courtesy car	Curtis Seacarr
Debit card	Deb Bittcard
Gargoyle	Garr Goyle
Gay bar	Gay Barr
High deductable	Heidi Ductable
Less is more	Les Izzmoore
Lowest price	Lois Price
Lowest offer	Lois Toffer
Martinizing	Martin Nizing
Maxed out	Max Dout
Maker	Maye Kerr
Near enough	Neera Nuff
Nickel and dime	Nick Kullendyme
Patent pending	Pat Inpending
Policy	Paula Cea

ORIGIN OF NAME	NAME TO BE
Politics	Paula Tikks
Politician	Paula Tishion
Primo price	Primo Price
Renting	Rhen Ting
Renter	Rhen Turr
Ripped off	Rip Doff
Rock quarry	Rock Quarry
Roll of dimes	Rolla Dymes
Roll of quarters	Rolla Korders
Roll of nickels	Rolla Nichols
Roll of pennies	Rolla Pennies
Rush delivery	Rush DeLivery
Sell my car	Selma Carr
Sell my house	Selma House
Sell my stock	Selma Stock
Sign over	Sy Noaver
Trade it in	Tray Diddin
Trade out	Tray Dout
Will reconsider	Wilrey Cunnsitter
Exact change	Zack Chainge

Employment (options & circumstances)

ORIGIN OF NAME	NAME TO BE
I need a job	Anita Jobb
Baker	Bake Kerr
Barber	Barb Burr
Berry picker	Barry Picker
Bartender	Bart Ehndurr
Bartending	Bart Tending
Bailing hay	Baylon Hay
Bare minimum	Bear Minnimum
Bell boy	Belle Buoy
Bell hop	Belle Hopp

Bell ringer	**Belle Ringer**
Builder	**Bill Durr**
Brick layer	**Brick Layer**
Cash his paycheck	**Cassius Paycheck**
Coal miner	**Cole Miner**
Correlate	**Cora Late**
Correspondent	**Cora Spondent**
Cost of living	**Costa Living**
Cotton picker	**Cotton Picker**
Demoted	**Dee Moated**
Delegate	**Della Gate**
Designate	**Dez Ignaite**
Dig her grave	**Digger Grave**
Dock hand	**Dock Hand**
Dock my pay	**Dock MaPaye**
Eligibility	**Ella Jabillity**
Errand runner	**Erin Runner**
Earned a living	**Ern DeLiving**
Earned income	**Ern Dincumb**
Earn a living	**Erna Living**
Earn a paycheck	**Erna Paycheck**
Earn a raise	**Erna Raze**
Forest ranger	**Forrest Ranger**
Itemize	**Ida Mize**
Co-pilot	**Ko Pilot**
More money	**Moe Money**
Omega man	**Omega Mann**
Auto mechanic	**Otto McCannick**
Owing money	**Owen Money**
Painstaking	**Payne Staking**
Painter	**Payne Turr**
Ran to work	**Randa Work**
Reassessment	**Rhea Cessment**

Redesign it	**Rita Zighnitt**
Shape up	**Shea Pupp**
Stevedore	**Steve Adore**
Typist	**Ty Pisst**
Waiter	**Waite Turr**
Wayne right	**Wayne Wright**

INSIDE THE HUMAN BEING

Agility, Strength & Posture

ORIGIN OF NAME	NAME TO BE
Arch her back	Archer Back
Bending	Ben Ding
Burly	Burl Lee
Dexterity	Dex Territy
Drooping	Drew Ping
Duke it out	Duke Itdout
Early years	Early Years
I lean backward	Eileen Backword
I lean forward	Eileen Forward
Firming up	Furman Nupp
Firm and strong	Furman Strong
Gaines strength	Gaines Strength
Gaines weight	Gaines Waite
Holding on	Holden Awn
Holding off	Holden Noff
Holding steady	Holden Steady
Holding still	Holden Still
On her back	Honor Back
On her hands and knees	Honor Hanzinease
Horizontal	Horace Zontull
Lean on it	Lee Nawnit
Leaning	Lee Ning
Lean in	Lee Ninn
Lean over	Lee Noaver
Lean out	Lee Nowt
Lean a lot	Lena Lott
Lean a little	Lena Lyttle
Manly man	Manley Mann
Over weight	Ova Weight

Posing	Poe Zing
Rock solid	Rock Solid
Rocks and teeters	Roxanne Teeters
Sitting	Sid Ting
Slim and slender	Slim Menslender
Slide out	Sly Dout
Slide over	Sly Dover
Squeaky joint	Squeaky Joint
Standing	Stan Ding
Tough enough	Tuff Finuff
Tough it out	Tuff Itdout
Will to live	Wilda Liv

Anatomy

ORIGIN OF NAME	NAME TO BE
Adam's apple	Adam Zapple
Angel face	Angel Face
Anatomy	Ann Atomy
Arm and a leg	Armand DeLaige
B cup	Bea Cupp
Bare ass	Bear Asc
Bare legs	Bear Laigs
Bow legged	Beau Legged
Boner	Beau Nurr
Birth of her child	Bertha Verchild
Boys and girls	Boyce Sengirls
Buck teeth	Buck Teeth
Butt ugly	Bud Duggly
Butt hole	Bud Hole
Calcium	Cal Seeyum
Dandruff	Dan Druff
D cup	Dee Cupp
Deltoid	Del Toid

Dick stiff	**Dick Stiff**
Dick's enormous	**Dixie Normous**
Donor	**Doan Nurr**
Urinating	**Eura Nating**
Fat ass	**Fat Asc**
Fatty tissue	**Fatty Tissue**
Goose pimple	**Goose Pimpl**
Guys and gals	**Guy Zengals**
Hands down	**Hans Down**
Hairy balls	**Harry Balls**
Hairy dangler	**Harry Dangler**
Hairy legs	**Harry Laigs**
Hairy palms	**Harry Palms**
Hazel eyes	**Hazel Isze**
Huge ass	**Hugh Jasc**
Human	**Hugh Mihn**
Humongous	**Hugh Munguss**
Gender	**Jenn Durr**
Genitalia	**Jenn Natailia**
Gestation	**Jess Tation**
Lean and mean	**Lee Nenmean**
List her cup size	**Lister Cupsize**
My keister	**Mike Keester**
My clitoris	**Mike Lyttoris**
My cock's big	**Mike Oxbigg**
Misty eyed	**Misty Eide**
All of her senses	**Oliver Senses**
Pearly whites	**Pearlie Whites**
Filled out	**Phil Dout**
Pinky finger	**Pinkie Finger**
Pip squeak	**Pip Squeak**
Quintuplet	**Quinn Tuplett**
Rosie cheeks	**Rosie Cheeks**

Rosie palms	Rosie Palms
Smiley face	Smiley Face
Cyclops	Sy Clopps
Tally wacker	Tally Wacker
Tiny dangler	Tiny Dangler
Toe nail	Tone Nail
Varicosity	Vera Cossidy
Vitality	Vi Tallity
Vitalize	Vi Tulize
You're enormous	Yori Normous
Your cock's big	York Oxbigg

LEAVING REALITY BEHIND

Drugs (help & hindrance)

ORIGIN OF NAME	NAME TO BE
I need a fix	Anita Ficks
Antibiotics	Anna Biodix
Antiseptic	Anna Septic
Antihistamine	Antti Hysstomein
Anti venom	Antti Venom
Barbiturate	Barb Itcherritt
Ben gay	Ben Gay
Burn out	Burn Nowt
Chap stick	Chap Stic
Chlorophyll	Clora Fill
Chloroform	Clora Form
Chlorinate	Clora Nate
Chloraseptic	Clora Septic
Cocoa cream	Cocoa Kreem
Codeine overdose	Cody Noaverdose
Cold remedy	Cole Dremitty
Cost enough	Costa Nuff
Date of expiration	Data Veksperation
Decongestant	Deacon Jesstant
Dextrose	Dex Trose
Floating	Flo Ting
Geritol	Ger Itdahl
Hypodermic	Hy Podermic
Joy ride	Joy Ride
Chemo therapy	Keemo Thairapy
Codeine	Ko Dean
Lay a pile down	Leia Pyledown
Lidocane	Lida Kane
Mello	Mel Oh

Melting	**Mel Ting**
Mix up	**Mick Supp**
Nicotine	**Nick O'Teene**
No more	**Noe Moore**
Orally taken	**Oralee Taiken**
Pain killer	**Payne Killer**
Pain reliever	**Payne Releever**
Filter	**Phil Turr**
Ripped again	**Rip Duhginn**
Roll a joint	**Rolla Joint**
Roll another one	**Rolla Notherwun**
Sky high	**Sky High**
Stoned again	**Stone Duhginn**
Soothing	**Sue Thingh**
Ti stick	**Ty Stic**

The Stupid, Rude & Generally Unattractive

ORIGIN OF NAME	NAME TO BE
Antagonize	**Ann Tagonize**
Bailing out	**Baylon Nowt**
BS'er	**Bea Esser**
Belittle	**Bea Lyttle**
Bull crap	**Bull Krapp**
Bully	**Bull Lee**
Buster keister	**Buster Keester**
Chance he takes	**Chancey Taiks**
Chastise	**Chas Ties**
Chicken shit	**Chick Kuhnschitt**
Clueless	**Clue Lis**
Daring you to do it	**Darren Youtaduitt**
Denting fenders	**Denton Fenders**
Eat and do little	**Eaton Doolittle**
You're a dick	**Eura Dick**

You're an asshole	**Eura Nasshoal**
You're an idiot	**Eura Niddiott**
Flipped out	**Flip Dout**
Held a grudge	**Helda Grudge**
Huge imbecile	**Hugh Jymbissol**
I'm a dick	**Ima Dick**
I'm an asshole	**Ima Nasshoal**
I'm an idiot	**Ima Niddiott**
Just an asshole	**Justin Nasshoal**
Just an idiot	**Justin Niddiott**
Lies a lot	**Liza Lott**
Lies a little	**Liza Lyttle**
Lies around	**Liza Rown**
Lot of crap	**Lotta Krapp**
Loud and obnoxious	**Lowden Aubnockshious**
Lie a lot	**Lyle Lott**
Lie a little	**Lyle Lyttle**
Malcontent	**Mal Cuhntent**
Marry in haste	**Marion Haste**
Know a secret	**Noah Secret**
Paltry	**Paul Tree**
Picked over	**Pic Dover**
Popped off	**Pop Doff**
Pop off	**Pop Oph**
Ripped up	**Rip Dupp**
Rip into it	**Rip Intuit**
Ripping	**Rip Ping**
Rolled into it	**Roald Intuit**
Royal pain	**Royal Paine**
Ruin a good thing	**Runa Goodthing**
Ruin another one	**Runa Notherwun**
Rush into it	**Rush Shintuitt**
Rude behavior	**Ruud BeHavior**

Stupid asshole	**Stu Pidassoal**
Tantalize	**Tan Tulize**
Teasing	**Tee Zing**
Tell each other off	**Telly Chutheroff**
Tear it up	**Terra Dupp**
Torn off	**Tor Noff**
Torn up	**Tor Nupp**
Tore into it	**Tor Rintuitt**
You aint nothing	**Uwe Nuttin**
Vivacious	**Vi Vaishious**
You're even stupid	**Yori Venstupid**

TIME TO HIT THE TOWN

Fabric, Apparel & Enhancements

ORIGIN OF NAME	NAME TO BE
Band box	Ban Box
Bobby sox	Bobby Sox
Braiding hair	Braden Hair
Cotton ball	Cotton Bahl
Cotton briefs	Cotton Briefs
Cotton pillow	Cotton Pillow
Crusty shorts	Crusty Shoarts
Curly cue	Curly Cue
Curly hair	Curly Hair
Diamond pendent	Diamond Pendent
Doily	Doy Lee
Draping	Drae Ping
Die her hair	Dyer Hair
Evening wear	Eve Ningware
Fading	Faye Ding
Fazing	Faye Zing
Fits my tush	Fitz Matush
Fits nicely	Fitz Nicely
Garter	Garr Turr
Glengarry	Glen Garry
Gunny sack	Gunny Sak
Handkerchief	Hank Kerchiff
Lacy briefs	Lacy Briefs
Leotard	Leo Tard
Levi jeans	Levi Jeens
Lot of static	Lotta Stattic
Loosen the belt	Lucinda Belt
Loosen the strap	Lucinda Strapp
Maxi pad	Maxie Padd

Make up	**Maye Cupp**
Make over	**Maye Koaver**
Mini pad	**Minnie Padd**
Mini skirt	**Minnie Skirt**
Mohawk	**Moe Hawk**
Nankeen	**Nan Keane**
Napkin	**Nap Kihn**
Nap sack	**Nap Sak**
Pair of shoes	**Paris Shues**
Powder	**Pau Durr**
Pearl necklace	**Pearl Necklus**
Penny loafer	**Penny Loafer**
Polyester	**Polly Ester**
Preston creased	**Preston Creased**
Red hair	**Red Hair**
Remnant	**Rem Nent**
Royal blue	**Royal Bleu**
Rhinestone	**Ryne Stone**
Sterling silver	**Sterling Silver**
Sizing	**Sy Zing**
Talcum powder	**Tal Cumpowder**
Taylor made	**Taylor Maid**
T shirt	**Tee Shirt**
Texture	**Tex Churr**
Tissue	**Tish Shue**
Ti die	**Ty Dye**
Wardrobe	**Ward Rhobe**

Transportation

ORIGIN OF NAME	NAME TO BE
A lane to drive in	**Alaine Todriveinn**
Ally way	**Ally Way**
Apollo mission	**Apollo Mission**

Cars and trucks	Carson Trucks
Chuck wagon	Chuck Wagon
Detour	Dee Tour
DeLorean	Del Lorian
Elevator	Ella Vader
Unicycle	Eunice Eickle
Ford motors	Ford Motors
Hale a cab	Hale LaCabb
Idling	Ida Ling
Generator	Jenn Nuraider
Lane narrows	Lane Narrows
Lincoln town car	Lincoln Towncar
Lease a car	Lisa Carr
Lease a Ford	Lisa Ford
Mack trucks	Mack Trucks
Manuel transmission	Manuel Transmission
More emissions	Maury Missions
Make and model	Megan Maudull
Mercedes Benz	Mercedes Benz
Motoring	Moe Durring
Mo-ped	Moe Pedd
Monroe shocks	Monroe Shocks
Monroe struts	Monroe Struts
Automatic	Otto Mattic
Auto parts	Otto Parts
Auto pilot	Otto Pilot
Auto repair	Otto Repair
Pop a tire	Papa Tyre
Park her car	Parker Carr
Filled up	Phil Dupp
Pick up	Pic Cupp
Pick up truck	Pic Upptruck
Red Wagon	Red Wagon

Regulator	Reg Youlaidurr
Rode a boat ashore	Rhoda Boatashore
Rode a bike	Rhoda Byke
Rode a horse	Rhoda Hoarse
Rotary power	Rhoda Reapower
Rick Shaw	Rick Shaw
River raft	River Raft
Rowing boats	Rowan Boats
Rush hour	Rush Hour
Ride her bike	Ryder Byke
Ride her horse	Ryder Hoarse
Sky cab	Sky Cabb
Start up	Starr Dupp
Starter	Starr Turr
Stick shift	Stic Shift
Test model	Tess Maudull
Test ride	Tess Tride
Trailer	Tray Lurr
Truck ramp	Truck Ramp
Truck repair	Truck Repair
Truck stop	Truck Stop

LET'S GO EAT

Food & Beverage

ORIGIN OF NAME	NAME TO BE
Alcohol	Al Cohal
Anchovy	Ann Chovy
Anheuser-Busch	Ann Hysserbusch
Artesian	Art Teashun
Bagel	Bae Gull
Baileys and coffee	Bailey Zencoffey
Baileys and cream	Bailey Zencream
Beverage	Bev Ridge
Bleu cheese	Blue Cheize
Budweiser	Bud Weiser
Caesar salad	Ceasar Salad
Chardonnay	Char DeNaye
Chili dog	Chili Dawg
Chili pepper	Chili Pepper
Chuck roast	Chuck Roast
Cocoa butter	Cocoa Butter
Cocoa leaves	Cocoa Leeves
Colby cheddar	Colby Chedder
Colby longhorn	Colby Longhorn
Cottonseed oil	Cotton Seadoyle
Crisp and flaky	Crispin Flakey
Curly fries	Curly Fries
Frankfurter	Frank Furtirr
Ginseng	Gin Singh
Goose berry	Goose Barry
Hazel nut	Hazel Nutt
Head of lettuce	Hedda Lettuce
Honey mustard	Honey Mussturd
Carrot juice	Karat Joose

Carrot stick	**Karat Stic**
Kaiser roll	**Keizer Rohl**
Kipper snack	**Kip Persnak**
Lemonade	**Lem Inade**
Loaf of bread	**Lofa Bread**
Lumpy potatoes	**Lumpy Tatoes**
Linseed oil	**Lynn Seadoyle**
Macaroni	**Mack Coroni**
Mayonnaise	**Mayo Naize**
Making bacon	**Megan Baycun**
Melba toast	**Melba Toast**
Miller beer	**Miller Beer**
Minestrone	**Minna Stronney**
Olive pit	**Olive Pitt**
Olive oil	**Olive Voile**
Olympia beer	**Olympia Beer**
Olympia brewery	**Olympia Brewery**
Patty melt	**Patty Melt**
Pepper corn	**Pepper Corn**
Pizza pie	**Pete Suppighe**
Pop corn	**Pop Corn**
Poppy seed	**Poppy Seed**
Porter house	**Porter House**
Red pepper	**Red Pepper**
Reuben sandwich	**Reuben Sandwitch**
Rich coffee	**Rich Coffey**
Romaine lettuce	**Romaine Lettuce**
Romaine noodles	**Romaine Noodles**
Rose of corn	**Rosa Corn**
Rhubarb	**Rube Barb**
Scotch and water	**Scott Chenwater**
Scotch and soda	**Scott Chinsoda**
Shelled and salted	**Sheldon Saltidd**

Salting	Sol Ting
Cider	Sy Durr
Triscuit	Tris Kitt

Fruits & Sweets

ORIGIN OF NAME	NAME TO BE
Bear claws	Bear Claws
Buster bar	Buster Barr
Candy bar	Candi Barr
Candy coated	Candi Coated
Candy corn	Candi Corn
Candied apple	Candi Dapple
Candy cane	Candi Kane
Candy Kisses	Candi Kysses
Candy store	Candi Storr
Chips ahoy	Chip Zahoi
Cookie dough	Cookie Doe
Craving cookies	Craven Cookies
Crusty pie	Crusty Pie
Duncan donuts	Duncan Doanitt
Dutch apple	Dutch Apple
M & M's	Emma Nemms
Frosty freeze	Frostee Freeze
Georgia peach	Georgia Peach
Ginger bread	Ginger Bread
Ginger snap	Ginger Snap
Graham cracker	Graham Crackurr
Heath bar	Heath Barr
Honey bread	Honey Bread
Honey butter	Honey Butter
Honey comb	Honey Comb
Honey do	Honey Doo
Ice cream	Ice Kreem

Icing	Ice Singh
Marshmallow	Marsh Mello
Patty cake	Patty Cake
Peppermint	Pepper Mint
Pear tree	Per Tree
Pie crust	Pie Crust
Pop sickle	Pop Sickel
Poppy cock	Poppy Cock
Red apple	Red Apple
Reese's pieces	Reece Espieces
Rich flavor	Rich Flavor
Rock candy	Rock Candee
Rocky road	Rocky Rhode
Semi sweet	Semi Sweet
Sugar candy	Sugar Candee
Sugar coated	Sugar Coated
Sugar cookies	Sugar Cookies
Sugar and spice	Sugar Enspice
Sugar cane	Sugar Kane
Whip cream	Whip Kreem

Who's Doin' The Cookin'?

ORIGIN OF NAME	NAME TO BE
A meal you cook	Amelia Cook
A meal you eat	Amelia Eat
A meal you serve	Amelia Surve
A meal in itself	Amile Linitself
Baking	Bake King
Barbeque	Barb BeQue
Belching	Belle Ching
Burner	Burn Nurr
Carry out	Carrie Out
Chili bowl	Chili Bohle

Cookie jar	Cookie Jarr
Cookie cutter	Cookie Kutter
Delicious	Dee Liscious
Delicatessen	Della Cattesson
Dining	Di Ning
Dine in	Di Ninn
Diner	Di Nurr
Dicing	Di Singh
Eating out	Eaton Nowt
Eating right	Eaton Wright
Hardy appetite	Hardie Appatight
Ice box	Ice Box
Ice chest	Ice Chest
Catering	Kay Durring
Marinade	Mare Inade
Mason jar	Mason Jarr
Mixing bowl	Mick Cingbole
Nutritious	Newt Triscious
Pan to cook in	Panda Cookihn
Pizzeria	Pete Sirria
Pizza cutter	Pete Zakutter
Pop bottle	Pop Boddle
Salivate	Sal Ivate
Salt shaker	Salt Shaker
Seal a meal	Sela Meal
Shelled and sealed	Sheldon Sealed
Slicing	Sly Singh
Spike the punch	Spike DePunch
Stew pot	Stu Pot
Tato peeler	Tato Peeler
Tasting	Taye Sting
Tea cup	Tee Cupp
Weight watcher	Waite Watcher

Whipped up
Will power

Whip Dupp
Wil Power

THINGS TO BUY, THINGS TO FIX

Retail Manufacturing

ORIGIN OF NAME	NAME TO BE
Antenna	Ann Tenna
Aerosol	Aris Saul
Bill shredder	Bill Schredder
Bobby pin	Bobby Pihn
Camcorder	Cam Korder
Crystal chandelier	Crystal Chandelier
Curtain rod	Curt Enrod
Garbage can	Garr Bijcan
Hope chest	Hope Chest
Humidor	Hugh Mihdohr
Jack O'Lantern	Jack O'Lantern
Closet door	Klaus Zyttdoor
Coaster	Ko Sturr
Linoleum	Lynn Noalium
Magnet	Mag Nett
Matricide	Matt Trespadd
Neoprene	Neo Prein
Oakley	Oak Lee
Pan to pee in	Panda Peeyinn
Peerless faucet	Peerless Fossit
Penny weight	Penny Weight
Radio	Ray Dio
Reel-to reel	Real Tuhreel
Rubidium	Rube Ittyum
Samsonite	Sam Synnite
Shag carpet	Shag Carpet
Chandelier	Shanda Lier
Sky light	Sky Lite
Stick pin	Stic Pihn

Siding	Sy Ding
Textile	Tex Tile
Thermostat	Thurm Mustatt
Type writer	Ty Pryder

Construction, Tools & General Maintenance

ORIGIN OF NAME	NAME TO BE
AC-DC	Acie Deacey
AC power	Acie Power
Alan bolt	Alan Bolt
Alan Wrench	Alan Wrench
Axe will fall	Axel Fall
Axel grease	Axel Greece
Band saw	Ban Saw
Bent and broke	Benton Broke
Bent and leaning	Benton Leening
Building	Bill Ding
Built to last	Bill Tulast
Branding iron	Brandon Iron
Kerosene	Cara Sein
Case box	Case Box
Sharpening	Char Pinning
Conduit	Conn Duit
Douche bag	Deuce Bag
Dig her up	Digger Rupp
Emory board	Emory Board
Emory cloth	Emory Cloth
Gauging	Gay Jingh
Hack saw	Hack Saw
Hall way	Hall Way
Juck hammer	Jack Hammer
Coating	Ko Ting
Lariat	Larry Aht

Leaking	**Lee King**
Leeway	**Lee Way**
Leverage	**Lev Ridge**
Loosening	**Lucen Ning**
Loosen the bolts	**Lucinda Bolts**
Peg board	**Peg Board**
Phillip screwdriver	**Phillip Screwdriver**
Power surge	**Powers Surge**
Rocks and debris	**Roxanne DuBree**
Rustic	**Russ Stic**
Rusting	**Russ Ting**
Rusty nail	**Rusty Nail**
Rusty steel	**Rusty Steele**
Surge protector	**Serge Protekturr**
Shaping	**Shae Ping**
Simonize	**Simon Isze**
Stanley tools	**Stanley Tools**
Tree house	**Tree House**
Turn her off	**Turner Roff**
Tie down	**Ty Down**
Wainscot	**Wayne Scott**

LIVING AMONGST THE LIVING

Kingdom Of Animals

ORIGIN OF NAME	NAME TO BE
Alligator	Al LaGaidurr
Ally cat	Ally Katt
Angel fish	Angel fish
Anteater	Ann Teeter
Ants in his pants	Anson Iscpants
Ants and spiders	Anson Spiders
Bee hive	Bea Hive
Billy goat	Billy Goat
Bob cat	Bob Katt
Bunny hop	Bunny Hopp
Bunny rabbit	Bunny Rabbit
Caribou	Cara Booh
Cat bird	Cat Byrd
Cat fish	Cat Fish
Chipmunk	Chip Munk
Coral snake	Coral Snake
Dalmatian	Dal Mation
Dodo bird	Dodo Byrd
Dinosaur	Dyna Soar
Elephant	Ella Funt
Fat pig	Fat Pihg
Guard dog	Garr Dawg
Golden retriever	Golden Retreever
Goose down	Goose Down
Goose eggs	Goose Eggs
Goose feathers	Goose Feathers
Gregarious	Greg Alrious
Gypsy moth	Gypsy Moth
Heard of cattle	Herta Cattle

Honey bee	**Honey Bee**
Hybrid	**Hy Brid**
Eat your own off spring	**Ichiro Noffspring**
Jack ass	**Jack Asc**
Jack rabbit	**Jack Rabbit**
Jay bird	**Jay Byrd**
Caging	**Kay Jingh**
K-nine	**Kay Nine**
Kitty cat	**Kitty Katt**
Lady bug	**Lady Bug**
Leonine	**Leo Nine**
Malamute	**Mal Lamute**
Martin gale	**Martin Gale**
Marine life	**Maureen Life**
Nanny goat	**Nanny Goat**
Nat's ass	**Nat Sass**
Nest her eggs	**Nester Eggs**
Panda bear	**Panda Bear**
Pollywog	**Polly Wawg**
Queen bee	**Queen Bee**
Red Snapper	**Red Snapper**
Robin's egg	**Robin Zegg**
Rhinoceros	**Ryne Noscurrous**
Rhino	**Ryne Oh**
Salamander	**Sal Ammander**
Salmon	**Sam Munn**
Centipede	**Senta Peed**
Shell fish	**Shell Fish**
Snake pit	**Snake Pitt**
Spider web	**Spider Webb**
Spring chicken	**Spring Chicken**
Star fish	**Starr Fish**
Starling	**Starr Ling**

Tad poll	**Tadd Pole**
Pterodactyl	**Terra Dackdull**
Tiger paws	**Tiger Paws**
Tiger shark	**Tiger Shark**
Toy poodle	**Toi Poodle**
Tom cat	**Tom Katt**
Tree frog	**Tree Frog**
Unicorn	**Una Corn**
Vixen	**Vic Sun**
Wildebeest	**Wilda Beast**
Wiley coyote	**Wiley Kiotey**
Wolf hound	**Wolfe Hound**
Wolf pack	**Wolfe Pakk**

Living With Plants

ORIGIN OF NAME	NAME TO BE
Ambergris	**Amber Griss**
Branch out	**Branch Chout**
Butch wax	**Butch Wax**
Chickweed	**Chick Weed**
Chrysanthemum	**Chris Anthemum**
Clover leaf	**Clover Leef**
Clover leaves	**Clover Leeves**
Coral reef	**Coral Reef**
Daisy chain	**Daisy Chane**
Dandelion	**Dan Delion**
Emerald forest	**Emerald Forrest**
Emerald green	**Emerald Green**
Fern tree	**Fern Tree**
Floral arrangement	**Flora LeRaingement**
Gardenia	**Garr Deenia**
Harvesting	**Harv Vesting**
Hedge clippers	**Hedge Klyppers**

Herbarium	**Herb Airium**
Herbaceous	**Herb Aishious**
Herbivore	**Herb BeVore**
Holly hawk	**Holly Hawk**
Huckleberry	**Huck Uhlberry**
Ivy walls	**Ivy Walls**
Jewel weed	**Jewel Weed**
Lily pad	**Lilly Padd**
Lily pond	**Lilly Pond**
Linsey-woolsey	**Lindsey Woolsey**
Magnolia	**Mag Nolia**
Marsh land	**Marsh Land**
May flowers	**Maye Flowers**
Ming tree	**Ming Tree**
Oak tree	**Oak Tree**
Pal meadows	**Paul Meadows**
Periwinkle	**Perry Winkle**
Pete moss	**Pete Moss**
Filbert tree	**Phil Burttree**
Rain forest	**Rain Forrest**
Red rose	**Red Rose**
Rhododendron	**Rhoda Dendrun**
Rose bud	**Rose Budd**
Rose bush	**Rose Busch**
Rose garden	**Rose Garden**
Rose peddle	**Rose Peddle**
Sage brush	**Sage Brush**
Sequoia forest	**Sequoia Forrest**
Sequoia tree	**Sequoia Tree**
Spring flowers	**Spring Flowers**
Stickley	**Stic Lee**
Summer flowers	**Summer Flowers**
Vivarium	**Vi Verrium**

Violets are blue
Wilting

Violet Zahrblue
Wil Ting

PRIVILEGED, POWERFUL & THE BIBLE

Prosperity, Wealth & The Fortunate Ones

ORIGIN OF NAME	NAME TO BE
Billionaire	Bill Yenair
Co-dependent	Cody Dependent
Dow Jones	Dal Jones
Fond memories	Fawn Memorees
Glory days	Glory Daise
Golden outlook	Golden Outlook
Handsome fellow	Hans Sumfella
Happy days	Happy Daise
Lead a good life	Lita Goodlife
Living good	Liv Engood
Live forever	Liv Forever
Live on and on	Livan Ehnawn
Loose and free	Lucen Free
Lucky number	Lucky Number
Lucky stiff	Lucky Stiff
Marry and multiply	Marion Multiply
Married again	Mary Duhginn
Married her	Mary Durr
Marry into it	Mary Intuit
Matrimony	Matt Tramoany
Mating	Maye Ting
Making history	Megan History
Met a good girl	Meta Goodgirl
More to gain	Morta Gain
Notoriety	Nota Riotty
Priceless	Price Lis
Raise a family	Ray Zahfamily
Wrote it off	Rhoda Doff
Rich bastard	Rich Bastard

Rich guy	**Rich Guy**
Scott free	**Scott Free**
Simplicity	**Sim Plicity**
Sunny disposition	**Sonny Disposition**
Troy ounce	**Troy Ounce**
Tycoon	**Ty Koone**
Wins her heart	**Windsor Hart**
Wins her love	**Windsor Love**

Race, Religion & Royalty

ORIGIN OF NAME	NAME TO BE
Adam and Eve	**Adam Meneave**
Anti Christ	**Antti Kriest**
Arch bishop	**Arch Bishop**
Aristocracy	**Aris Talkrussy**
Believer	**Bea Leever**
Beaner	**Bea Nurr**
Chaplin	**Chap Lynn**
Cherokee nation	**Cherokee Nation**
Cherokee tribe	**Cherokee Tribe**
Cheyenne nation	**Cheyenne Nation**
Cheyenne tribe	**Cheyenne Tribe**
Chicano	**Chick Awno**
Christian burial	**Christian Berriel**
Christian wedding	**Christian Wedding**
Destiny awaits	**Destinee Awaits**
Destiny child	**Destinee Child**
Dolly Lama	**Dolly Lama**
Ebony and ivory	**Ebony Ehnivory**
Emigrate	**Emma Grate**
European	**Eura Peeyan**
Faith healer	**Falthe Heeler**
Fair and equal	**Faron Niekwull**

Hinduism	**Hind Dewism**
Holly Holy	**Holly Holy**
Hope and pray	**Hope Penpray**
Christianity	**Kristie Anity**
Kneel down	**Neil Down**
Kneel and pray	**Neil Lenpray**
Nobel man	**Noble Mann**
Paul bearer	**Paul Bearer**
Polynesian	**Paula Neishun**
Philippino	**Phillip Peeno**
Praise the lord	**Praise DeLord**
Priest hood	**Priest Hood**
Priestly	**Priest Lee**
Prince charming	**Prince Charming**
Roman catholic	**Roman Kathlick**
Rastafarian	**Ross Tifarien**
Royally	**Royal Lee**
Salvation	**Sal Vashun**
Scarlet night	**Scarlett Knight**
Unify	**Una Fye**
Worldly	**World Lee**

LOVE OR SIN?

Sex & Pornography

ORIGIN OF NAME	NAME TO BE
Ate off all of her bush	Adolph Oliverbusch
Ate it out	Aida Dout
Androgynous	Ann Drodgenyss
I feel your dick	Aphelia Dick
I feel you licking	Aphelia Liccun
Bury the bone	Barry DeBohn
Boning	Beau Ning
Bing banger	Bing Banger
Boy does girl	Boyd Uzzgirl
Breeding	Brea Ding
Bulging	Bull Jingh
Bust her cherry	Buster Cherry
Bust her hymen	Buster Hymann
Bust her open	Buster Roapen
Chastity belt	Chastidy Belt
Craving more head	Craven Moorehead
Dick goes in you	Dick Gazinia
Dick in straight	Dick Instraite
Dick straight	Dick Strait
Dig her hole	Digger Hoal
Dominator	Dom Minader
Domineer	Dom Minier
Dug deep	Doug Deep
Early riser	Early Rhiser
I leaned over	Eileen Dover
Them are some big ones	Emerson Biggens
Them are some nice ones	Emerson Nyzons
Fits my bush	Fitz MaBusch
Gargantuan	Garr Gantshuinn

Hankering	Hank Kurring
Held a dick	Helda Dick
Huge erection	Hugh Jureckshun
Hung well	Hung Well
Chasing pussy	Jason Pussee
Lean him over	Lena Moaver
Lot of love	Lotta Love
Lovie dovey	Lovie Duhvey
Lucy gucy	Lucy Gucy
Moan a little louder	Maona Lyttlelowder
Made out	Maye Dout
Making love	Megan Love
Moan a lot	Moana Lott
Moaner	Moe Nurr
Need a stiff	Nita Stiff
All of her clothes off	Oliver Kloazoff
Oral sex	Orel Secs
Palm her breast	Palmer Breast
Fill his hole in	Phyllis Hoalynn
Red light	Red Lite
Rock hard	Rock Hard
Rocky romance	Rocky Romance
Shacked up	Shaq Dupp
Take it all off	Tae Kidauloff
Tiny package	Tiny Package
Whaling away	Waylon Nuhway

JOIN UP NOW

Membership Required

ORIGIN OF NAME	NAME TO BE
Den mother	Den Mother
Festivities	Fes Tivitees
I'm a member	Ima Member
Ivy league	Ivy Leegue
Genteel	Jenn Teel
Joining	Joy Ning
Join in	Joy Ninn
Join up	Joy Nupp
Junior division	Junior Division
Junior varsity	Junior Varsity
Note of approval	Nota Vahprooval
Pow wow	Pau Wau
Pen pal	Penn Pal
Posting	Poe Sting
Royal wedding	Royal Wedding
Ceremony	Sara Moany
Scout leader	Scout Leeder
Scout master	Scout Master
Summer camp	Summer Camp
Sign in	Sy Ninn
Sign off	Sy Noff
Sign out	Sy Nowt
Sign up	Sy Nupp
Validate	Val Idate
Verify	Vera Fye

Printed in the United States
By Bookmasters